WHAT'S
the STORY?

WHAT'S
the STORY?

Reflections on a Life Grown Long

Sydney Lea

GREEN WRITERS PRESS *Brattleboro, Vermont*

Printed in the United States

10 9 8 7 6 5 4 3 2 1

Green Writers Press is a Vermont-based publisher whose mission is
to spread a message of hope and renewal through the words and
images we publish. Throughout we will adhere to our commitment to
preserving and protecting the natural resources of the earth. To that
end, a percentage of our proceeds will be donated to environmental
activist groups. Green Writers Press gratefully acknowledges support
from individual donors, friends, and readers to help support the
environment and our publishing initiative.

Giving Voice to Writers & Artists Who Will Make the World a Better Place
Green Writers Press |Brattleboro, Vermont
www.greenwriterspress.com

Visit the author's website at: www.sydneylea.net

ISBN: 978-0-9909733-9-3

PRINTED ON PAPER WITH PULP THAT COMES FROM FSC-CERTIFIED FORESTS, MANAGED
FORESTS THAT GUARANTEE RESPONSIBLE ENVIRONMENTAL, SOCIAL, AND ECONOMIC PRACTICES
BY LIGHTNING SOURCE ALL WOOD PRODUCT COMPONENTS USED IN BLACK & WHITE,
STANDARD COLOR, OR SELECT COLOR PAPERBACK BOOKS, UTILIZING EITHER CREAM OR WHITE
BOOKBLOCK PAPER, THAT ARE MANUFACTURED IN THE LAVERGNE, TENNESSEE PRODUCTION
CENTER ARE SUSTAINABLE FORESTRY INITIATIVE® (SFI®) CERTIFIED SOURCING

For Stephen Arkin and Fleda Brown,
with boundless thanks and affection.

Contents

2. DEJECTION

3. THE BEAST IN THE JUNGLE

Contents

Prologue

You learn a thing or two by getting along in years, or so it's claimed. My poor, cursed friend Sammy, dead so young, didn't get a chance to test such a claim. He crashed his motorcycle, or rather, a car smashed it for him. I suppose that's another story.

But Sammy may in fact belong in this one, because, after all, he was my dearest friend for some years. He was also and always his doting grandmother's pet. I knew the old woman well, a sweet-as-pie lady if ever one lived. Is that another story too, or stories, plural? Anyone's personal history doubtless comprises subplots galore; who can be sure which is pertinent?

In any case, I'm sitting here waiting to see a doctor for some minor emotional problems. I've visited him now and then over quite a span of time, though never about anything that made him or me or anyone believe I was on the cusp of crisis. Just a little unease, that's all. You might roughly liken this appointment to an oil check.

The waiting room's walls are yellow, and that could be behind what's going on with me just now. Despite the flowers on their corner tables, that color invades me. It makes a solo hunting trip come rocketing out of my far past, because on my way home, all but out of gasoline near midnight, and with nowhere open to replenish the tank, I spent some doleful hours in a Maine motel whose walls were painted this very same yellow.

I'm sure the building was something much different back when the town thrived. The clapboard frame house may have taken boarders, say; but later a flat-roofed row of rooms, jutting out from its rear side into a former pasture, had been added. I wouldn't be surprised if that extension were torn down by now, the big house restored and turned into a bed and breakfast, as has been happening for some while to so many of these old New England home places, so grand and so tired. An out-of-towner buys one, spruces it up, then hangs a quaintly lettered sign, usually with some name meant to be evocative but in fact absurd: "Quail Acres," maybe, in a part of the world where quail never existed, or similarly, "Elk Meadow," or else something romantic story-bookish—"Sherwood Forest," "Midlothian," what have you?

In the autumn I recall here, the town didn't have much left but a paper mill, itself close to extinction, much of the industry having already moved south to places with cheaper labor: Arkansas, Mississippi, and the like. I took the room, having no real choice, though I knew it would be full of an unmistakable mill-stench. Almost fifty years later, merely to think of that sulfurous reek makes me queasy, not to mention actually smelling it as I pass through one of the few towns where mills have survived, however shakily.

To the point: that night in the motel I felt that I was doomed somehow, that nothing would ever come to good for me. Why such melodrama? I couldn't and can't make sense of it, because in fact my life was pretty average at twenty-five, neither particularly happy nor otherwise. Still, the restless tick-tick-tick of my young dog's paws on the scuffed linoleum floor made it seem ten *years before morning broke and I could go find fuel. That clatter from a nervous pointer sounded like a prelude to judgment.*

As it happens, when I sat down in the doctor's office a few minutes ago, I took *Psychology Today* from a table, finding an article there by a certain Dr. Silver, who opined that a person normally mourns a dog for three weeks. Well, I've buried a fair number of dogs since that night I recall, and whenever I think about one, no matter how long he or she has been dead, I almost weep. On every one of them, be it pet or hunter, there hangs more than one tale.

Of course I don't weep, not really, not out loud, as my friend Sammy's grandmother did off and on until the day she died herself.

Was I abnormal? I can't say. At all events, that night I pictured a chasm yawning before me, and I felt certain one day I'd fall into it. And so I did in a way, though at length I'd climb out on the other side, or mostly out, as I've said. I'll talk about that at some other point. It's hard enough to stay on track here.

What made a night in a yellow motel so taxing? What about it induced this vision of the abyss? That particular dog was, if anything, too alive. Sammy still blithely trod the earth—or maybe not blithely, but he did move around on it for certain. Yet somehow I knew, or believed I knew, there was something terribly wrong on that earth, and it involved an evil act or thought of mine, even if I couldn't for the life of me have described the what or when or how of my transgression.

I remember a train's passing through that patch of village. It must have furnished the moribund mill. The freight cars' clanking and rumbling woke me around daylight, and the engine's whistle seemed to scream misery and condemnation of my ineffable sin.

I'd keep on living with this kind of vague anguish for years, still unable to give it a name. Things are better for me now, much better, but to this day it abides, for the most part all but imperceptibly. Still I feel hopeless to work out a narrative when so essential an ingredient goes unidentified, even if I have all those others. The spooked dog's paws. My long-gone boyhood chum. His sobbing grandma. The train. The stink of the pulp mill. What do I know of psychology? What does anyone know?

That I ended up with the wife of my dreams and with five good children and five grandchildren so far—well, all that is simply a wonder. It can't be explained. It surely can't be told to a doctor, not if I can't tell it right to myself.

I mean, what's the story, really?

Whatever
I
Might
Say

WHATEVER I MIGHT SAY

THOUGH TO TOUCH ITS FLAME would surely be as painful as when it burned brighter, the candle's low now. On the table, just prior to guttering after dinner, it vaguely illuminates friends.

The glow takes me to Creston MacArthur, one son's and one grandson's namesake, and to our many evenings as a campfire ebbed. Just now I'm remembering a particular night, the two of us seated next to a favorite river, swapping stories. His were better.

A bleakness sinks into me despite the patent pleasures of this supper interlude with other people I care for and admire. I've long savored their camaraderie, their conversation, their gifts for wit. The lateness of the hour has turned our talk to rote murmuring, something like the water of that river, which always flows right below my consciousness.

I should do more now than merely prattle with these good companions, just as I should have said more to Creston, gone almost forty years, and perhaps he to me. Or maybe not: deep in the woods, barred owls started to chatter that night. "Like a good pack of hounds," Creston said, and that woodsy locution seemed perfect, seemed pinpoint accurate. I smiled.

Still I'm unsettled. It's as though I were looking on these people here, on my children, on my children's children, on my past—I'm looking from above. Having failed to put the right words together, I've risen over our group like smoke.

The chill in my spirit has something to do, I'd venture, with feeling removed, and feeling removed because I'm tongue-tied. And I'm tongue-tied for fear that any speech of mine will sound formulaic.

It's late. The guests will leave. The candle's wick whispers. I must hope I've found a way of being with loved ones that's better than any talk I could grope for, than any I craved as those old fires grayed, a way that bespoke me better than whatever I may have said, whatever I might say now.

FORGIVENESS

MY FOURTH GRADE TEACHER abused me at every turn, no matter I was a good kid—or maybe not that, but in any case not really a bad one.

Once, for example, the man accused me of writing some wise-guy story, when truth was, I meant only to compose a comic one. Sneering, he read it aloud to the class to demonstrate my unpardonable irreverence. I still hear his voice, deliberately turned mousey; I see his curled lip as he speaks. As I say, all I'd intended was comedy.

Believe me, I found no humor in what he called me the morning after my commonplace playground tussle with my good friend Monty, during which Monty fell and dislocated a vertebra in his neck. That meant he'd die, I knew, and I cried all night at the prospect of his death but equally of my own. Everyone understood that such a crime meant the electric chair. It was all so unjust: I'd meant no harm at all. You couldn't even have called it a fight. No one felt angry.

Thank God, Monty came to school the next day, wearing a big cervical collar. He also wore a grin—a bit self-conscious but genial—as if nothing unusual had happened. No matter: that sadistic schoolmaster called me "Man-Killer" in front of everyone, which reduced me to tears again. My reaction wasn't logical, because there my friend was, sitting at his regular desk. Yet the preceding night's emotions, especially after so little sleep, had lingered, barely under the surface.

By now, the tyrant who often beat me, who constantly humiliated me in front of my friends and, far worse, enemies like George Piglio and Billy Legrand, is doubtless long dead. No matter, I find myself looking for an old-fashioned curse. I'm sure none has ever really worked, but I'll give it a try anyhow.

Wherever he is, may my old teacher wear a collar like Monty's, but lined with biting insects, and may someone yank it up over his head, abrading his ears as he did mine when I tried on my new peewee football pads, excited right after they'd been issued in the gym. Let someone rip the collar off, thrust it on again, rip it off, on and off, the bugs feasting, forever and ever, amen. Let someone magically turn *him* into a child for a spell, then lay on all this punishment in reprimand for normal childish behavior.

But no: here I am, come to think, flinging invective back his way over sixty years and more, even though he's surely long dead, and I, still alive, having purged such spleen at last, should be able to pray, as I do, that he rest in peace—the bastard.

MAYA

July, 1955 in a hot, brown field, whose only indication of
life is the grasshoppers' rattle. People are calling out a *name.*
I see bits of clothing for *bases,* a lump of cloth in dirt for
home. A gray boulder, unreliable backstop, slumps behind the
catcher.

It's a fight to recall these terms, not to mention that the
contest has something called *innings:* whichever team can
score a greater number in nine is called *winner.* I come to
recognize all this for a moment, but yes, it takes an effort. In
a brief spell of clarity, I notice that the members of one team
are sulking. They must be *losing,* as people put it.

It all seems oddly present, though memory's thinner
than mist. Nonetheless I know that back then I felt as if I were
peering from under the eaves of my skull, or someone's skull,
onto an utterly strange, unfamiliar scene. Things were going
on out there, but everything appeared immaterial, props in a
sort of shadow play.

Voices kept repeating a name in chorus: they seemed to
think it was mine, but what or whom could mine signify?
Whomever they called was expected to come grab a bat, its
wood slick with others' sweat, then swing it at a ball.

Did those others mistake my hesitation for self-regard
or for contempt of their fun? They taunted me, cursing how

slowly I walked across the stubble field, and then how I idly watched an object sail from some farm boy's grip. Three times it streaked near me, then past. I heard the jeers, but faintly, as if from great distance.

I record all this because just now I felt something akin: I beheld a hand reaching inside a bin for a scoop of dog food, and wondered to whom the hand belonged, and what *belonging* could indicate.

Another day was starting. There were whimpers of a dog expecting to be fed, the thump of its tail a hollow, empty sound. Outside a window, nondescript birds stalked insects in a meadow umbered by summer heat. A kitchen's sheetrock walls dissolved into pallor. A wife and daughter, as some call them, lay sleeping somewhere upstairs.

That old *I* surely heard those catcalls at his listless arrival and his careless turn at bat. "Just who do you think you are?" someone shouted. He noticed the gnats that hovered above the field, and higher, the vultures, to which he gave no meaning whatever. The wheat had been shorn by machines, so that even through their shoes some must have felt rough stubble, but in memory, he did not. A figure—*I*? someone else?—had approached *home*, which was no more than a jersey flung onto the earth; apart from that pocked, minor boulder, it was the only halfway solid thing in view.

FOOL'S DAY

APRIL 1ST. I SCOUT THE HAZE, all hung with birds, and from height-of-land I survey the face of the mountain off to my east, its snow leached away but for two or three ribbons of gray. All I'd like to see etched on what I behold, as if it would justify me—as if it would be a sort of poem carved into the blank of snow—is vanished as well.

I turn downhill on a long dead farmer's path, which invades a barn. The building writhes astride that lane, while inside, the frost that changed dirt floors to marble has melted. A primitive tractor under the empty mow wears lusterless, olive-drab paint.

Why try for stoical thought, distilled and lean? Such effort is inevitably brought to nothing by my senses, which exert their idiot sway: I probe a cobweb funnel with a mittened fist; I taste the piquancy of ancient hay; I smell the must of powdered animal dung; and I swear I hear the paper banners cry out from chestnut rafters, *Army Air Force. Keep 'Em Flying!* The banners go back to the '40s, the rafters much farther.

I climb onto the tractor's crackling saddle and grip the wheel, its wood still blanched by dead men's sweat. I imagine their hands, like some I've long since thought I'd shrugged off for good. They held my shoulders lest I fall like a soldier. The men with the hands had been in the military themselves for the most part. Home after the second great war, they gripped the lathered reins of Warrior Maiden, my Shetland pony, as, bit in mouth, she loudly sucked from a rippling trough. I wanted the reins to myself. *I* wanted to play the highland warrior.

Sentimental now, I'd welcome hands that also enveloped mine on a tractor's wheel, kept softballs and footballs flying, and must have laid me down in the crib. "Too soon old, too late smart," my grandmother used to say.

I'd best leave right now, before my boots sink deeper into muck.

From their mud-clad nests in the eaves, the springtime swallows leap down to strafe me.

ADOLESCENCE

What do they want from me? Standing by the small beaver pond in his home woods, he recalls asking the question of empty air.

The *they*—changed or gone. Likewise, the *he*—or perhaps so.

All this time later, an April breeze cuffs at him, cooling the sweat of a walk among trees, lifting and drying a few lonesome strands of hair. He regards the marsh pond's water. What is out there? Anything? If not there, where?

That morning in his fifteenth year had begun slowly, the slowness part of what would enrage him. The boy sneered down at his place mat's nursery-rhyme inscription, meant to delight the little child he'd long since outgrown. Pale orange pulp floated in his cup. Eggs gummed his dish, their very yolks looking bleached; one of his long bangs had fallen athwart the mess, so low did he slump in his moping.

In the kitchen, as ever, Nana plied her mother-of-pearl brush and spoke her mealtime grace. Even in dank summer, he could hear the crackle of her electrified tresses above the drone of her prayer. His mother's mother, she had always lived with them (and always will, he sometimes cursed).

In a corner clucked the grandfather clock, which never told the right hour. The thing was probably intended to lend some elegance to the house, but it appeared clumsy and squat to him. The tuneless chimes referred to nothing. Locks streamed over all quadrants of its face—blown by the four personified winds. How fat, each beaming visage!

Thud thud thud. His bald father came mumbling downstairs, too cheerfully, and then his mother, equally heavy of gait, hair soggy from bathing. One sister, already there in what they called The Breakfast Nook, was spooning up wet Wheaties and reading the words on the cereal box, rapt, as she twirled a pigtail with chubby fingers.

One thing and then another.

No breath of air.

It was August, everything laden, the leaves swollen thick, and the shadows. Pompadours of diesel exhaust formed over tractors that slowly combed the neighbor's field, flushing hordes of dun grasshoppers into aimless arcs. Grape vines hung sinuous, hairy. Under the bay window, he saw the usual knot of escaped steers, tearing at the brown-spotted lawn, and grimaced to see the ticks and botfly larvae on their shaggy pasterns. Fitch, the Nubian goat, stood on the roof of the Plymouth pickup, his beard green with grassy spit. This daily antic had once seemed funny.

The boy idly picked at the clot of yolk in his own coarse mane, then looked away to the one small portion of the Nook's beige wall that showed no imbecile knickknacks on shelves, none of Nana's crude watercolor landscapes.

By now two younger brothers and another sister were seated, blearily conning the tabletop. So when a question landed from somewhere—"Why don't you cut your hair?"—it may not even have been directed at him. Furious anyhow, he flung his fork: it skittered the length of the room. He noted the small ligament of foodstuff it left on a baseboard, then the family members' expressions as he sped away. They looked more puzzled than alarmed, so he paused on the porch for one more bellow, all vowel, before trying to slam the door, on which dull claws had inscribed their desultory trails over the years. The door's heavy wood seemed almost to sigh, though, shutting slowly with a minuscule pop. The brass dragon knocker wheezed itself horizontal, settling back with a faint click.

Their burr-matted spaniel heaved from the porch's floorboards, deaf and trustful. She sidled over, favoring bad hips: would there be a walk? The boy cursed, swinging his foot near her. The dog half-fell down the three steps and limped along at heel, indifferent to his intended cruelty, her naïveté deep, galling.

The spaniel, eyes scarcely more functional than the rest of her, soon deluded herself that a dusting pigeon was catchable prey, and bumbled toward it. The bird flapped lazily onto a crab apple branch, and the dog, her charge died off into an indifferent gaze, posed in benign paralysis amid the smears of prematurely fallen fruit on the driveway. The boy sneaked behind an unbarbered hedge and made his way toward the slough.

The hills were swathed in haze thick as shaving cream. It would be ninety degrees and humid by noon. Frogs torpidly twanged in the reeds. The familiar smells of baked mud and vegetation honed his anger. He beat at the muck with a dead-fall branch, which broke almost at once. He continued his savage assault with fist and elbow, over and over. The algae blooms parted with every blow, then instantly re-gathered. Two bumblebees choired dull harmony around a clump of limp jewelweed.

There wasn't any way out. Everything blurred as he looked back over the lawn. *Go face the music*, he thought. Then he winced and spat the word aloud: "Music!"

He wanted somehow to be watched, to have his mind read, though his mind remained unreadable, even by him.

Now he remembers a sudden wind's rising. Clean-edged, it wiped off the haze, stropped the shadows, and no matter that he's inclined to skepticism (the breeze just happened along), he is equally given to some form of credence (those gusts were meant to be). The wind entered his world from nowhere, like a presence he'd invoked.

And more miraculous still: out where the water lay deep—at least to the eye of a child, even an irritated adolescent—a fish slashed at the surface with its tail, coursed the length of the pool, and disappeared. Probably a sucker, he surmises today: only a big trash fish, but in this moment so many years back, an apparition akin to the meteors that now and again ignited the summer sky. The burnished scales on its flank looked as vivid as such a fall, or as chips of mica had once seemed when he found them glinting in quartz and prized them free. The fish-scales shocked back the forenoon's rays, however fleetingly. Or, there being this motif to the day, he remembered the swirl and gleam of the barber's pole in the village, which had signaled something both fearsome and seductive when he was led past it and inside for the first time.

These decades later, he shies a twig into the beaver pond and chuckles. He is wiser now, or ought at least to be. The chuckle fades to a wry smile. How could he have known back then in his unfathomable rage that his hair would thin and his figure would thicken—like a plot?

He'd never have prophesied these after-moments, which would wait for ages, and then come at him in a rush more sudden than the sucker's. So far from resenting them, he'd come to cherish his elders for having trodden certain paths before him, for helping him to tread his own, a path in some ways so strange in his eyes and yet somehow so blessed that his heart beats daily thanks for it.

You come to understand some things, he supposes, from having children of your own. When his daughters and sons were little, when they nattered or fumed, he needed—as he couldn't have guessed, either, those decades ago—to pray for some animating reference. He needs it to this day: some flash, some silvery flume.

SEX AND DEATH

I HESITATED, DOUBTFUL I REALLY WANTED to learn just what that racket could be, mere yards into the woods behind our house. Hilarity seemed to blend with loud despair in that caterwaul, a mix that struck me somehow as expressive, though I couldn't have said of what.

Uncanny. The word flew into my thoughts unbidden. Once you dig up its roots, of course, it really means nothing more than unknown, yet in common use it often holds some hint of horror.

I longed to go indoors, unhorrified, where fall's first fire waited in the woodstove. Now that the house had lost its children, I looked forward as well to a romantic, last-of-the-workweek meal with my wife. I wanted to get away from . . . what? a windigo? a werewolf? Nothing ordinary, at all events. I couldn't associate that hullabaloo with any local fauna, which I know thoroughly.

My flashlight found two forms, not big, not small, the size perhaps of new fawns, but far darker—dark as dark ever was. I saw an eye-gleam, then another, and finally four, each the color of a coal: two porcupines, carnally clinched, hooting and cackling. I still can't think quite how to describe those squalls.

My childhood hero Frankie Farrell once showed his own eyes' glint and, laughing meanly, proclaimed he wanted to die at what these beasts were so roughly up to. I wasn't quite sure what he meant, though I recall managing a comradely, pseudo-manly chuckle. Frankie, twice my age, could knock men out. He could walk on his hands. He could do a back flip from a standstill.

A porcupine, however, is not even good at climbing the trees that make up his diet, so these two looked awkward in their noisy act of sex—or maybe just careful, as in the lame old joke. Indeed, they chattered their teeth and tittered as if their behavior were, exactly, a sort of petty fooling around.

But then they'd hiss like bobcats, or scrabble, or bark. Graceless, ugly things. I considered the hours I'd spent over the past summer, pliers in hand, plucking quills from my swift but stupid bird dogs, all yelp and twitch and tremble, their blood flecking our mudroom. So perhaps it was simple rage that drove me now, though surely that's too simple a description.

When I got a little closer to Frankie's age, my very first sweetheart and I would chafe and claw at each other's bodies, as if we meant to do each other harm. Ignorant, near-savage erotics.

I ran to the shed, grabbed a shovel, rushed back, and clubbed that pair of animals dead. It takes some doing to murder creatures with brains the size of warts, but it's not as though I wanted violence, only peace and calm.

As I quelled one set of noises, however, others rose to mind: the wails of sirens; the deafening whistles of great churning trains; the shrieks of taloned raptors; the clamor of enraged men. I heard them all, uncanny.

MRS. RAGNETTI
AND THE SPIDER

STILL WARM THIS MORNING, autumn's chill yet to come. An angler spider, trailing its thread, precisely, like a fishing line, has just caught me, in perfect coincidence with my random recall of *la signora Ragnetti*. In memory, the woman remains the ogre who terrified me every Thursday afternoon all through a winter. At singing lessons, fist on high, she led me, barely turned tenor, through cheerless versions of *"Caro mio ben"* and others. My mother had sent me to her. I've tasted hell. It is with me now in present tense.

I arrive, cradling my folio of airs, sopped and stained by the smutty snow of this stranger's land, the asphalt city. The bells of San Cristofero's drone a torpid portent of the agony ahead. It seems I hear the teacher even before I knock on the door: "How is this? You do not do these things I tell you, so simple. *O Dio, che stupido . . .*"

The spider must think he's found arachnid heaven: that is, if a spider may be said to think. He surely considers me quite a catch, not knowing how I've shrunk. He's likely drunk with joy, unaware of how in those old sessions, when (*cretino! farnullone!*) failure seemed its own long season, I was hollowed out to a specter. If the spider tweaked his thread, I'd rise. I'm only air in this nightmare, a whiff of ether.

How can Mrs. Ragnetti, at five feet and perhaps ninety pounds, appear so huge? She wrests the door and impatiently waves me in, clicking her tongue. "So different from my son," she growls, before I've even removed my spattered jacket. She turns to study the son's photograph on a table. A middle-aged man stares out, face set and stern as her own. She crosses herself, scowls, then sits malignly down. Soon, too soon, her left hand jabs at scales on her piano, the right one clamped in that gnarled fist, as if she held a dagger.

"*Piu forte!*" she insists. I flinch, as though from actual blows, while we *do-re-mi.*

"*Desastro!*" she spits while I grapple up and down those ladders, no matter that I know my voice, however timid, finds the pitch of each note exactly: "Do you come to me for making a noise?" Another note, another Latin imprecation. I grow colder, colder—and smaller. Once I've returned home, I know my mother will reject any complaints as self-pitying, puling, craven. She's been assured that *la signora* is the region's premiere voice coach. Am I not up to excellence?

Released at last, I cross the street to buy an icy milkshake, laced with malt, scant consolation for all I've felt go out of me. It's an effort directly counter to reason: the treat, rather than numbing me, seems to freeze even harder the fear I'd meant to melt, the poisonous residue of terror, hate.

Once I felt the ruthlessness of la Ragnetti. Now a spider imagines he'll lift me into his maw.

JERRY, SOLITARY

OUR NEIGHBOR IS ALMOST NINETY, and she's the one I'm visiting. She's Jerry's neighbor too, and he's the one I'm watching out the window. Fifteen years old, country to the bone, he's there in the chill shooting baskets, trying to play some inner city black kid. His get-up is ludicrous. Hoodie. Bling. Sagging trousers. The boy's expression and his moves are meant to suggest both control and indifference: a fluid leap, an easy spin, a follow-through, his hand dropping as smoothly as if he pulled a window blind.

But why the act? How would Jerry suspect he was being studied? Surely he imagines his solitude to be absolute.

Out of sight in the barn, his father must stay busy with the milking machines. I hear them drone. Life goes on. Jerry's mother, I've been told, has rented a double-wide trailer down by the bridge. I don't judge. Back thirty-some years, when I had a son near Jerry's age myself, I too got divorced.

You'd think a kid like Jerry would be angry. My boy was. You'd expect him maybe to pound the ball between shots, but his dribble's lazy, random, and his face looks almost dreamy. If the rusted rim had a net and I were outside, closer to him, I'd hear *swish* after *swish*. He's accomplished, all right. It might do him good to play for our small school's team; and they could use him.

My aged neighbor is, as ever, hard on Jerry's mother. "Her husband gave his family *everything*," she insists, shaking her head, wattles quivering.

I don't answer, since I'm not certain if she means to imply disapproval of the wife's behavior only, or to include some censure of Jerry's appearance too. His underpants show above the belt of his fat-legged pants, his head's clean-shaven, he may picture himself with neck tattoos.

I visit because our neighbor is rheumy, half-deaf, and failing by the month. Life goes on.

How recently it seems the old lady was hale, and the boy a sweet blond baby. And I? Turning into an elderly man is the biggest surprise of my life.

Like any such kid, no doubt Jerry hopes his parents will reconcile.

Darkness settles, only the far mountaintops still bearing light. He can't know I watch him there as he paces off an NBA three-pointer, twenty-three feet from the backboard—or in this case the side of the barn, which could stand some tending. It's late November, the dooryard earth hard as ice. I want to look away. Jerry must realize his long shot won't go.

It will never go.

BLACK MARKS

ON THIS SUNDAY MORNING IN MARCH, I've been walking the Snake Road, its tar prematurely dry; our winter was small this year. I kneel to consider twinned, dark marks on the pavement, snake-like themselves. They were probably made last night by some adolescent burning rubber, as my buddies and I used to say when we were beer-crazed boys.

I won't continue another mile or so to the turn where a beater Ford Ranger went out of control a decade and some ago. A pair of kids—the one named Willy driving, Evan his passenger—slid across the macadam and smacked into a pine. My wife, to whom I'd been married only twelve years back then, was heading the other way in the very next car to arrive, our two-year-old daughter with her. How sadly different my life would have been if that pair had turned up mere seconds earlier.

Wife and child watched Willy as he shook his friend by the shoulders, crying, "Evan, Wake up!" Evan would not wake up.

I rise to my feet and feel my stomach pitch. How sadly different too some other lives might have been if a certain child had walked ten feet more closely behind the small, car-chasing terrier I ran over at seventeen. I see that girl clearly, mouth gaped in a wail. I think of the fear that must have gripped her mother, who knelt behind her clutching a trowel.

Spring's familiar flocks of geese have begun to course over. Their yelps sound woeful enough, yet the birds strike me as icons of life. Those that survive the weather and shotguns will come by again in late October. I imagine an autumn rain, this buckled roadbed a welter of mud and yellow leaves, the same sound overhead once more. I will smell that chamois odor of decaying sweet fern, which certifies the absolute finale of summer.

I sometimes think we endure, if we do, by accident. Evan's drunkard grandfather had given the under-aged boys their liquor. One afternoon, years earlier, the old man knocked his wife out cold on the broken ground where she tended her flowers. Or so I once heard from Luther, the wretched couple's son, like his own wretched son gone to a too-early grave. Luther, black sheep among black sheep, overdosed on Oxycontin, and Evan gone now too. The sins of the fathers, indeed, as it is written.

Today's March 1st, which happens to be my wife's birthday. By now there have been twenty of which she might not have been conscious, nor that daughter either. I turn from these tracks on this tiny roadway, having been reminded how everything in this world awaits a defining moment.

MISTERIOSO

JOHN ORE STOOD HIS BASS UP, Frankie Dunlop laid his sticks on the snare, and they walked offstage. Thelonious Monk stayed on hunch-shouldered, hit a note with one finger, then stared at his keyboard a long, long time. Another note, another drawn-out gaze, and another, others. He did not rise to whirl as he often would when he played this club, or any. He didn't smile, benign, as he always smiled when dancing.

Monk wore some African beanie—I mean no disrespect, Lord knows. I just don't know what you'd call it. His face beneath it looked both blank and rapt.

I was rapt myself, as I'd been for the whole first set, and in fact for years even then, but for different reasons, I'm sure, from Monk's, whatever those may have been. I believed he was speaking to *me* somehow, that he knew my inmost sorrows and expectations. I guess a lot of people thought that.

I was looking for eloquent mystery in those odd plinkings, which may have been there, though if so, not in a way I could fathom. With the noise of chatter and movement, I couldn't possibly have heard my heart, *lubdub*. But I did.

Later, after the last set ended, he sat on the same way, playing lone notes as if contemplating just where each came from. *Right there in front of you!* I wanted to shout.

Who knew that in front of him too lay those decades in which he was close to speechless, his piano hushed, until he died like anyone else, though he was not like anyone else?

But I don't want to riff on what I dreamed Monk meant to my life, so small and young, comprising only things that any man that age is bound to go through. I don't want to get all full of lyric triteness, smoke-softened light glancing off the bottles behind the bar, sorrowful looks of his sidemen—who may just have been puzzled or annoyed—as they left him.

It was 1963. I won't go into history, or politics, or whatever else might make something grander than they truly were of my thoughts.

There was only Monk. There was sound, then quiet.

CATCH

WHOEVER YOU MAY BE, stop reading now if too much sentiment, no matter how genuine, makes you uneasy or angry or whatever else. If you do hear me out, however, I hope you're not the sort who'd say that my good wife throws like a girl, as my Little League baseball coach once claimed I did, the moron. I threw just fine until my arm got robbed by age. That happened some time back, to be sure.

You don't have to remind me I might have known worse losses.

Whoever you are, go stand beside my wife, at exactly sixty feet, six inches from some target, and then by God we'll see how many times she can take a ball or even a stone and hurl it, and how often she'll hit the can, the post, the tree—and then we'll see how often you do. Good luck, sucker.

No, wait a minute. There's little reason to start all this in anger at you, whom I probably don't even know. I won't pretend I'm not angry, but why lash out at a stranger? It's doubtless only despondency that makes me talk this way.

I've now and then pictured my wife playing catch with the one boy in her five-sibling family, the one who fought cancer for twelve years and died this past Christmas. I loved him, which is no doubt a crucial factor in my behavior here, my rhetoric.

I've seen photographs of those two kids, gloves on left hands, half-smiling, squinting under a summer sun, decades and decades ago. They were a good-looking pair in those days, and both were handsome into late adulthood, no matter most of his hair had been robbed by the vile, stinking chemo, and some of his teeth.

My wife recalls how, in the warm months, when they got home from school, the two would head right out to their yard to toss the baseball around and chat away the afternoon. For me, that's the very picture of innocence and affection, and if you, anonymous you, consider it the stuff of Norman Rockwell or Hallmark, just haul your sorry self off.

There I go again. Forgive me. I'm just uncertain which emotion is which here. For all I can really say, you were innocent too, and still may be, or at least known as a decent, caring person, and it's not after all as if I have some corner on innocence myself. Sometimes I reckon I've never been any better than I have to be.

For one thing, I probably should have been paying closer attention to my wife's brother—and to my wife as well, come to think about it. Not that it does anyone a bit of good when I beat myself over the head for my omissions. That doesn't change a thing. If it could, I'd keep at it forever, as in some respects I suppose I have.

On those long-gone afternoons, my wife learned to throw like a man. Instead of moping and cursing, I wish I were man enough to report all this and not break down. But do I really? Do I want to be manly by that definition—furious, fearless, unwilling to take any quarter or give any? There are better things to wish for. I know that these days.

My brother-in-law and I used to go down and watch our Red Sox play at Fenway Park. After a while we had daughters and sons, and we'd take them along. Home runs, triples, double plays: we roared approval at these and more; but we all, child and grownup alike, especially loved those bullet throws that Dwight Evans delivered to cut runs off at the plate.

Too soon, it seems, our lives just seemed to get too busy for Fenway. Then the god-awful cancer showed up. Starting in my brother-in-law's colon, it got to traveling elsewhere afterwards, and the whole time I only sat here and typed words, as I'm doing even now, weeping. Meanwhile my poor wife is sick with sadness, and I wouldn't blame her if, thinking back to those old summers, she picked up something and threw it dead-center between God's eyes.

THE TOUCH

—in mem. Jimmy Smith (1925-2005)

I HAD JUST PARKED IN FRONT of the general store when the jazz DJ proclaimed, "There was only the one Jimmy," and so when I heard the too-blue sounds of "When I Grow Too Old to Dream" on my radio, I knew what was up, and turned blue too, and sighed a long sigh.

Late-winter slush sprawled on the pavement, and the world for that spell seemed so *cold*. But at last I went in to where Maggie stood behind the counter. She's my friend, and is always cheerful, and that revived me a little. I noticed her hands, for one thing, and how lovely they looked as she took my dollar and tapped at the register. I stood right there and drank her store's good coffee.

I left, hands on my mind. I thought back to an earlier show that day, which had featured a woman whose company manufactured robotic vacuum cleaners. Now she was making bigger plans: dishwashers, lawnmowers, cars—and of course the military was in touch. I bet it still is. As a little child, the woman claimed, she'd seen R2-D2, that bleeping machine in the first of the *Star Wars* movies to put me to sleep, and she "just went bonkers." Now she envisioned robots that would search through houses, defuse bombs, and go kill The Enemy, la-di-da. "And so," she said without irony, "those gadgets will keep a lot of people alive"—as though *people* existed only on our side of any conflict.

Then another guest came on to discuss how Internet banking had become the hottest web activity, apart, that is, from downloading pornography. I thought, no muss, no fuss: make whoopee or make a bomb and get quick bang for your buck, no hand to stop you. I shivered.

My own small buck for coffee had come of scribbling a check, which I'd handed to another friend, Paula, the local bank teller, earlier in the day. She and I spoke of the weather's recent nastiness, of how quickly our kids had grown and gone, of how they were doing well anyhow. But another neighborhood farm was set to go under. She wished she owned the bank and could cover the farmer's debts. I wished that too.

On the road home, I couldn't help recollecting a night from a lifetime ago, with Stanley Turrentine on sax, Donald Bailey on drums, Kenny Burrell on guitar, and Jimmy on Hammond B3 at Pep's Musical Bar in South Philadelphia, where I sat watching as much as hearing, a place about as far away in all respects as I could be right now. But oh, what I'd give to sit by that bandstand again as Jimmy's elegant fingers punched out their riffs and fills, the bebop lines crossing and mixing and fighting with the soul-blues stuff, because, Lord, there was such *life* in those hands! And no matter I was only a phony white brat in my stupid funky shades and was furthermore underage for that club and that best of organ-side tables and the whiskey sours I kept knocking back—no matter all that, I'd declare to this moment that a palpable blue rose into that room, for which reason, though I was alone, I wasn't lonely.

Short on courage, I didn't try to shake Jimmy's hand, but even if this Vermont is, yes, miles and miles and miles from that night in that corner club, I've kept the notion of him as my friend. And somehow he is, if only because he touched me once and it's with me still, the touch.

STONE ROLLERS

—for Don Metz

AT THAT STAGE OF OUR LIVES, we scrambled up Smarts Mountain and any number of others: Demmick Hill, Holts Ledge, The Hedgehog Den, Mousley, Smith, Cottonstone, on and on. Having made our camps at the top, at some point or another one of us would say we could live like that forever.

All the seasons called us to those heights, but especially winter, when we could light as big a blaze as we wanted and could dance like imagined, aboriginal tribal people, the firelight bright as noon, our shadows shooting clear to the crowns of trees, high branches sagging with snow. Afterwards we sat by coals and said, perhaps, the best things we'd ever say to each other.

It's like yesterday. So goes the cliché, but my body at least knows better. I can still climb those old hills, but not so quickly. My friend Don has aged more robustly. Still, the two of us could never do the thing, strange as it was, we also did back then, because it would require a strength we both must admit has waned, as it inevitably will. We wrestled up great rocks and sent them down the steepest slopes we could find. Each boulder pulled hard from the frozen earth, but once it did, soon became a force that nothing—unless it were an even bigger boulder or a stout trunk that flashed an orange wound when all that weight struck it—could even slow.

A snowshoe hare once hopped aside just in time to save itself. Songbirds woke and flushed. Each understory shrub and sapling salaamed in the wake of power released by strong, young, reckless men, the boulders' speed and clamor enough to rouse whole neighborhoods.

All this was simply something that you'd do if like those young men you knew you could live this way forever.

DIZZY

TERRY AND I HAD PUSHED SO FAR INSIDE the hair-dense brush in that corner of Maine that he joked, "This place could scare a man to death." Of course he didn't meant anything by it. A saying, was all.

We had been chasing one wily grouse for miles, it seemed, but could never quite get a shot in those dismal woods. I didn't have the courage to say it, but from somewhere down in my soul, a place I try not to visit, just then a memory came hurtling in: I was a boy, inching along within a limestone seam, cheap flashlight clamped in one hand as I scrabbled with the other. I felt the same dizziness.

My aim, as so often in those years, had been to earn some fame among my friends and foes alike. I'd find the cave at tunnel's end, then report back to other boys who were all caught up like me in looking tough. I stopped short at the very first fork I reached, though, suddenly and terrifyingly aware of what *lost* might mean in a darkness so far underground. I had briefly snapped off the light and experienced the quintessence of black.

So out I backed, webs showing up in my beam, pale insects clenched in their strands like suspended souls. The tunnel-walls' chalk made avalanches so soft I dreamed more than felt them.

The recollection made no sense at first: here I stood in Maine, many miles from that limestone passage. I wasn't alone, either, but with one of my steadiest friends. *Thank God Terry's here,* I thought, but then to my shock I noticed an odd pallor in his face as we struggled along through the brush, wet clay gripping our boots. I saw how he staggered, just as I did, as if overtaken by the same spinning sensation.

I called out, "You all right?" Terry just shook his head. We felt whatever we felt.

It was all I could do to whistle up my bird dog Bessie. I leashed her, and we slogged back to the truck from that fathomless forest, which bog had repossessed, leaving only a scant few human traces: the rusted bail of a bucket, a plow blade, a sagging strip of barbed wire. Nature had returned to claim what had been hers from the start.

Now Terry is not like me, his mind rarely bolting to strange places. Fact is, I have long admired him as a man who holds to routine, to moving right along, Perhaps that's just what he did once we got back home. In any case, though it may seem odd, we almost never refer in any detail to that baffling scene, from whose unspecific threat we fled—just as, many years before, I'd wriggled backward out of a limestone tunnel, clutching my light, so minuscule and feeble.

MANNISH BOY

I RECALL THE MUDDY WATERS BAND when they played
The Postage Stamp. I knew Muddy's licks on guitar by heart,
James Cotton's on harp as well. I felt that I might have written
"Long Distance Call," for instance, by way of some magical
gift come down from my stars. To be tuned in like that, I be-
lieved, should show the world what I was.

I hope it's forgivable to have been so full of nonsense
when young.

I've become a man since that time, when I longed for
Muddy to acknowledge a white kid versed in his every song,
by title, lyric, recording session, a beer-brave kid who thought
he had *something* at least to offer. Though I wouldn't sing
and couldn't play, there'd have to be some reward for my de-
votion. The famous bluesman would see a chance when he
took his break to honor spiritual kin. With an inward eye, I'd
already pictured myself and my hero, the two of us sharing a
laugh and a drink, so that I'd also be heroic to the crowd out
there, if only by association.

The vision would soon enough die, not the first or last
one to do so.

Muddy had closed his set with "Mannish Boy" and now
he clearly had it in mind to be exactly that: he was sounding
some handsome, gold-skinned lady deep in a corner. I had to
settle for Muddy's drummer, an older man in brogans and an
age-sheened double-breaster.

The drummer had painted an owl on his bass. Years later, I wince at the stupidity of the question I asked him about it. Here, alone on my porch, I feel the Arctic blow into my soul, but it isn't weather that makes me shiver. It's the long distance call of recall. I was full of Utopian dreams back there in the sixties. I asked, what was signified by the painting?

Who-who-who-who: close by an owl starts up as if prompted. How different is life today? How different from back at that tiny club, when I expected—what? a tale of some Delta adventure? a discourse on Yoruba myth?

The chill in my bowels assures me, again, that I'm not star-crossed at all. I'm only what I ever was, an implausible dreamer who can scarcely believe in himself.

The old sideman questioned me back: "Tell me, son, you blind, or is you only lame-brain?"

That boy I was: he may look like a man now, but he's no less awkward than before.

"What I painted on my drum is a owl," said Muddy's drummer.

I'VE KEPT ON ANYHOW

— for Peter Fritzell

I STEP INTO OUR SPRAWL OF WOODS, where Zack and his
father used to hunt. Zack lately sent a block-printed letter to
thank us for those years of hunting permission—and to say
he won't be back.

He claims for him to hunt deer without his dad just isn't
the same: "ITS LIKE I SEE HIM WITH ME CLIMBING UP ON
BARNET KNOLL THEN I REMEMBER HES NOT."

≈

I hike downhill, straight into Zack's soul, or rather my own,
into times when I hunted smaller game in a bigger state with
my father. In my own mind's eye just now—and it's small
wonder—I see a day as fine as God could make, two years
before my father fell, like Zack's. Two gentle spirits.

Now a trick of memory summons a busted covey, flushing wild and well out of range ahead. The noon sun turns
those bobwhite into feathery splendors. How could we wish
any harm on them?

And yet, having watched several of the birds settle down
some few yards beyond a sprawling second growth of yellow
pine, we set out to make that bright flock rise again.

Dejection

THE SERPENT
ON BARNET KNOLL

THE YOUNG RETRIEVER noses a frozen snake across the rain-glazed snow. The creature should long since have wriggled deep into mulch in some granite fissure, so that when it died, it would do so down there, in secret. That it didn't seems odd.

But my mind's still odder, having followed its own inward paths from that coiled corpse to a moment this morning before I set out: at the mirror, greasing lips against the cold, I inspected myself. The age-lines, the puckering mouth, the thin gray hair—all still shocked me. I also studied a wen, the permanent swelling that puffs my left eyebrow into a small horn. It's the frozen snake that has reminded me of that passing moment, though how it did so I can't explain.

Out here, I encounter the morning's savage gusts. The spruce-tops thrash and complain. When there's a lull, I hear the ceaseless and meaningless scolding of red squirrels, the grating of ravens.

One day, in my third grade year to be precise, I knocked off Joe Morey's hat on the playground, taunting him for a sissy, even though he and I were friends for the most part. Nearly weeping with frustration, he reached down for the hat at the same time I did. Our heads clapped together, my brow swelling slightly but, as it turned out, forever. I'd meant to be cruel that day, I was, and I got my long-lasting due.

In life, the snake was a mere, harmless garter. Today it's something else, and makes me quit my hike for a while. I stand and wait, but nothing comes to change me. Why would I dream it would, no matter my unvoiced, uncertainly directed, all but unconscious pleading?

It's almost Christmas, a holy time for many. Through decades of northern winters, I've never seen a snake at large in December. But however I strive to discover something significant in the event, nothing reveals itself except what I've long known about snakes—mere facts, devoid of meaning, versions of reality that seem only somehow to discredit me.

Was this the creature's first cold season? Who knows? A snake doesn't count or reason. But I do; I know there are just so many moments in anybody's life. Why do I stand here statue-still and fritter a single one away? And yet what else should I be thinking about?

I have wife, children, grandchildren, along with a host of lesser earthly attachments. I clench them tight to my heart, but there come times when a sort of unattached self prevails. Left at large too, I know, that other self might contemplate violence or crime. Also, of course, it doesn't. I daily, dutifully, and gladly return to a bourgeois life. Am I not therefore absolved? But what in me requires absolution anyhow? I simply feel this unsettledness, ungovernable, random, opaque.

One day my head struck someone else's, but even before that, surely, something had slithered into my soul. It would linger lifelong, making subsequent, unwelcome forays up to the cool surface, whenever, however it might.

DEJECTION IN LATE WINTER

THESE COUNTLESS BUGS that dot the white beneath the south sides of trees—whose winter sheen I once believed a glory—leave me as cold as my own rote attributions to them of endurance and gumption.

I stoop and prod the snow fleas into action with a gloved finger. In field guides, they're called springtails, but no matter their names, they stir no more than my thinnest, most jaded, amateur interest. They're here come every late winter. If only they still called for my keen witness, not this languor and ennui. The predictability of the natural world seems dismally akin to that of my own rehashed responses.

I used to delight in the annual, vernal transformations, the climatic quarrels, new warmth pushing back at old chill, iced hardwoods full of sap, gravid does tiptoeing across the remnant ice of loosening brooks, thaws in wetlands drawing frogs and turtles up from their slumber in muck.

For now, however, even the snow fleas' bustlings, like my tired anthromorphisms, seem banal.

LAME AND SOUND

WHATEVER THE AILMENT, he wasn't right. You could tell that just by observation, however subtle and oblique I tried to make my own. I already knew of his infirmity, to be sure. He didn't live in our town, but I'd seen him before in that bigger one, where I go now and then to do errands. The least attentive person on earth wouldn't miss him, with his home-made walking stick, his filthy parka, the odd, fringed bandana he wears around his head, and above all the way he moves.

That morning, his cloth-wrapped head was conspicu-ous, precisely, in his tortured movement. Glancing sidelong, I could watch the bandanna's flapping as he performed a series of frenzied nods, staggering away from the magazine stand where he'd just bought some sort of sex magazine, maybe only *Playboy*, maybe something even more witless. In any case, he appeared desperate to vanish, to make for home, whatever home might amount to.

As for me, I'd just bought a copy of the New York *Times* in the little convenience shop. The place was crowded, but any who noticed him looked quickly away, as I say. No one wanted to behold him as he lurched to the hissing door, then through, humping himself along like some shot beast. No one wanted to imagine what he'd ever done, what he did now, what he might do once gone from our view.

For my part, while a fall rain, hard as a sledge, kept thumping the roof, I imagined the pouts of the magazine's back-cover models. I'd barely glimpsed the colorful advertisement before the lame man vanished, yet for some reason its glamorous couple, in their sleek, red, hide-seated convertible, regarding each other with smoldering eyes, had seared my brain.

The woman's expression was obviously designed to seem sexual, but to me—although, no, I wasn't able to look at it for much longer than a second—her face crazily resembled that of the reeling cripple himself: full of pain, even anguish.

As for the man in the picture, we were to understand that he could speed away at will, as some lithe, wild creature might, the sort of creature a car like his would be named for.

PASSING THE ARTS
AND CRAFTS FAIR

—in mem. Irving Chamberlin (1929-2011)

I READ THE SIGN ON THE FENCE, *Artists Can Heal the Planet,* and I think, *Oh no, they can't.*

With few arts of my own to rely on, I liked to visit Irv's shop, to watch him build a chair you could actually sit on. But I loved him, chair or no chair. There aren't many like him anymore, the soft-spoken old ones, who still know how to farm, how to raise up a house you can live in, how to still-hunt a whitetail. Of course, you have to break down their reticence, which takes patience, always well repaid. But even then, they play their parts in their own stories pretty humbly.

Irv dropped as he tilled the garden next to his and Marion's house on the river, where today his ivory potato flowers likely display their blooms in neat rows. The potato flowers would do for his funeral, lovely as they are—more so than whatever the artists may be displaying in their earth-healing fair. Not that I know that; I merely suspect it.

Irv's gone, and the earth keeps whirling, not to be healed for now, maybe never. Probably never.

How fine, that almost shy way the man would greet any-one he cared for, his smile barely perceptible, his ice-blue eyes cast down, his words hard to discern at first. Not that Irv was cold, only modest.

He was what he was, irreplaceable among other things.

The day is wind-raked, so Irv's weathervane rooster must be spinning like the planet in question. He may have wrought the vane himself, for all I know. It must point in every direction. Just to think of it is a grief.

HOW ABOUT SOME
QUIET IN THIS PLACE?

—May 2003

THERE WAS A CLEFT OF ROCK at our height of land that
made a perfect seat, so I sat. At dawn, I could see shadbush
and apple and flowering crab down in the village. There was
simply this *palette* before me, and everything ought to have
been as it ought.

Turkeys should have been gobbling, and calls of warblers
should have been boiling in the forest. And maybe in fact they
were, and maybe even the spring-swollen Connecticut River
had an audible, gentle *shoosh*. But for me that rush wasn't water at all. No, it was the mild roar of tinnitus, static at medium
volume with a ring in it like a tiny alarm.

I thought, how about some quiet in this place?

How about a little peace? My ringing ears made me
cranky almost to violence, but where would I direct any
violence? In mind, I took in the world, riddled with killers,
some all safe and sound in their DC offices, with their elegant
leather armchairs, brass lamps, and bold views onto sublime
landscape and monument. Meanwhile, in other towns, in hills
and deserts and jungles, hundreds and hundreds of people—
black, beige, brown, white, boys and girls too—ashes-ashes,
all fell down.

They knew no silence, no calm while the slogans joined
with general clamor: *Iraqui Freedom Mission Accomplished*,
and the like. I thought it again: how about some quiet?

Wild columbine hung on their stalks at my feet, and the wet-dog scent of newblown trillium floated upward to me from the bog behind, and I chewed some honeysuckle, to savor its petals' sugar. So I tasted and touched and smelled and saw, but I heard nothing besides my own inward current of rage, which was surely rage at clowns and murderers, all right, but also likely at every stupid, self-righteous act or idea I've ever entertained myself, maybe even my own sloppy fury in this place.

Though there was no quiet to speak of in these ears of mine, perhaps everything otherwise *was*, after all, as it ought to be. Black Angus steers and heifers on Paul Knox's farm below were grazing as they are meant to graze; I couldn't see the dung and mud on their flanks, so that from where I looked on they seemed clean and downright pretty, there in the green stretching abroad from the curious Shaker barn, round as a moon, while the river ran blue behind it, and beyond the river, New Hampshire's White Mountains, which made Ralph Waldo Emerson feel "like nothing."

True, at times I have wished I felt like nothing and so could make this ringing and this hurtle and outrage crawl out of my soul and off the ledge and slither down to the river and I'd be sitting there, Zen, impassive, unconnected to my senses, and might indeed be nothing; or rather, I have wished I could just feel something apart from this deaf, intractable anger.

To sit so, however, would be not to rise, as I soon did, and not to wander through the dew-drenched seedlings of pine, with their pastel beacons of growth at each tip, to the knoll above our home, from which I could gaze through a window at the face of one young daughter sleeping, and through another the face of her older sister, both surrounded by silence, no matter the roar, the slight awful roar in that place.

THE COUPLE AT THE FREE PILE

AUTUMN'S CHURCH BAZAAR IS OVER, all the stalwart, weathered tents of the vendors struck except the one over the White Elephant table. Early this Sunday morning, such tatty wares as went unsold still sprawl on the plastic tablecloth or on the ground, but the sign up front reads "FREE."

No car approaching or following, I brake to a crawl so I can observe a man and woman making their deliberate ways through the jumble. I naturally notice that their goods are gathered in the rusted bed of the wheelbarrow my wife and I donated to the event, which nods on its fat, limp tire like a weary draft animal.

For me to stop completely might be to embarrass this couple, who covet what we congregants had considered encumbrances. And yet, however it shames me, my curiosity—like desperate thirst, or lust—also impels me. I'll drive on, circle the village common, and pass back this way again from the other direction. After all, the two scavengers seem devoted to their scrutinies; I doubt they'll notice my second inspection.

I turn by a picket fence enclosing a big house's tidy lawn at the south end of the common. The owners held a well-attended garden tour there last June. Then I swing right again, north, going by the famous corner elm, which residents agreed at town meeting to save, approving a line item that funded the tree surgeons' services.

During the festival, I visited the White Elephant booth myself. As the saying goes, one man's trash is another man's treasure, and you never know. As I predicted, however, nothing appealed. Among other bits of uselessness, say, I found a basketball so worn it had lost all traces of its original, pebbled orange; three recumbent, saucer-eyed ceramic deer; a few chipped plates, inscribed *Disneyland, 1974* and showing portraits of Goofy, Donald. There were raveled rugs, tarnished lampshades and sconces, so on.

Passing the elementary school, I make a right again, and, before the turn that will take me to another view, I stop at the intersection, just opposite the village store. My wife and I will be having lunch there in an hour or so. Its deli is the best-stocked one for miles, the staff all cheerful.

As I drive, even more slowly than before, past the White Elephant display, I see a car seat in a Bondo'd pickup's cab. It holds a child, and he or she—it's hard to tell through the windows' grime—must have been sleeping a few minutes ago, but now I can just make out a mouth, gaped in a yowl I can't hear, even if I can imagine it. Surely one of the parents, or both, will step out of the tent to tend the toddler. For now, though, they stand motionless, one on either side of the wheelbarrow, eyes on me. Their stares are furious.

OLD COUNTRY SONG

MY PAL GEORGE AND I have been in recovery from booze for about the same span of time. The way he tells his own story, or stories, however, has for some reason always especially resonated with me. He remembers most vividly one particular night, and whenever he does, he says his guts twist again, and mine do too.

He was playing pool, and he reports that he'd lost all feel for cue and ball. He was shooting with this friendly Indian guy named Dee at a gin mill in Wyoming. It's easy enough to be friendly when you're robbing another guy blind. For the five hundredth time he'd run way over his limit of gin. He recalls that the racket inside the barroom seemed loud, then soft, like the sea when it washes in and out. He always shakes his head, which that night had turned to mush. Again.

He kept telling himself he could play this game, damn it all, if only his normal light touch hadn't flown south. Of course he knew it was wrong in the first place to be in that stinking hall, what with his wife back there at the Roundup Motel with their three-year-old son.

That morning the little boy had said, "Wyoming Friday is Japanese Tuesday." Maybe his wife had told the kid how time changes around the world. The child was heartbreak cute—and all confused. Who wasn't?

By George's account, a tiny rodent, one that could bite hard, hid under the clack of the balls and that ocean sound.

The critter felt like conscience: this had been meant for a family trip. Still, too many years would go by before the damned animal got real big and gripped his neck and sat him down, and chewed right into his pride and broke him but good. The rodent would hiss and growl beside him when that time came; he'd be holding a handle jug of booze in one hand, a gun in the other; he'd be thinking about how much easier things would be if he put an end to everything.

Just a few hours before the pool game, already wasted, his shaky morals gone, he'd tried to talk a barmaid into bed—or into his car, actually. But she'd had her eye on some other dude. So what the hell? He didn't want her. Not now anyhow.

All he wanted was the lightness of touch again. At various points, he swore he'd stay away from another drink just long enough to get himself straight and get back on his game, and that would mean this mess was over. He'd be there with the family, on vacation, out west. He flat *knew* the change he needed was coming, and soon. When it did, he'd take his money back and then some; every time he got beat he grew surer of that. It was nuts. He was nuts. So he might as well drink. He had to, of course. Christ, it was what he did.

He was too strong for the goddamned tight pockets, strong off the banks, strong each time he hit a lot-of-green shot. And he always seemed to get stuck behind the 8-ball. Dee, his two-hour buddy, kept on being friendly, but why wouldn't he be? Dee knew the touch was gone, if it ever had existed.

George had to be done with all this. Then he'd haul his sad ass back to his wife and son. But he kept drinking, putting the balls in the rack, sticking his glass on the rail, and setting himself up for good, hard breaks.

THE BIG IDEA

HOW COULD I KNOW the woman there with his father, her hair bleached almost sheer, the heels of her shoes as slim as pencils as she wobbled and pitched along the sidewalk—how could I be so sure she wasn't the poor child's mother?

But I did know. I could tell by the father's eyes. They snapped from his girlfriend to the boy, then ran up and down the crowded street, far side, near side. His face looked both panicked and empty, that mixed expression a boozer's face will take.

"Shit-fire!" I could hear the father curse. He had to be wondering, how had his kid gotten here, and why in hell just now? The two tawdry lovers must have picked this neighborhood, figuring it safe, far from either of their homes. Now this. Shit-fire.

No one would expect such a boy, maybe seven, to plead sophisticatedly, to offer a scolding long on rhetoric, as of course he didn't. He just stood there in front of the barroom, bewildered, screeching, "*What's the big idea?*"

Where *was* his mother? She couldn't be a saint herself, or her son wouldn't be wandering alone like this on the bad side of town, amid foot and motor traffic.

I could see the father was never meant to be fat. He must once have cut a good-looking figure. Fact is, he did even now, if you overlooked the beer-bloated belly that dropped down over his thin, white belt. His mistress must have overlooked it, after all, though she herself was well past any prime she may ever have known.

The New York Yankees *Y* on the man's cap was darkened to gray with age or maybe even mold. He tipped the cap back, letting go of his swaying sweetheart, then reached for his son, whose stiff-legged, backward scramble was enough to keep plenty of distance between them. Having chased for only ten yards or so, the man stopped, chest heaving.

I'd only come down here on errands, and not to this area at that; but it had simply been impossible to find a place to park my car a few blocks west, in the area to which I'd been headed just then, as quickly as my legs would carry me through this sordid block, littered with detritus, both animate and inanimate. Now I started to look for the missing wife as desperately as the drunkard, for other reasons than his. I wanted her not to appear with me for witness. I only wanted peace.

And then for no reason I daydreamed how, if I happen to hear cliché, I generally pay it small attention—until one suddenly lands someplace that gives it context, makes it compelling.

In this case, yes, what *was* the big idea?

That drunk wasn't ready to answer the question, or if he did, it seemed certain he'd say nothing to help his child, or anyone's. And so, momentarily delusional, I guess, I daydreamed of taking the poor boy by the hand and getting him to a quieter place. The big idea, I'd try to explain there, has something to do with human love. *Remember that*, I'd say, even though deep in my heart, in a place where darkness fights for space with other things, I was sick about mouthing an age-old saw that never held water to start with. Or at least that's the way I felt, there and then in my gloom. I'd read news that very morning of a fresh new slaughter. Some North African land. The usual scores of children in pieces.

A siren shrieked from a firehouse now, but, thank God, all it meant was twelve noon—which was instantly gone, though it would stay on, no doubt, for some time in one small head.

The boy seemed almost to like the phrase he'd shouted, no matter his tears, though *like* must scarcely be the word. Whatever the case, the question at least seemed right enough to him that he shouted it twice again—"What's the big idea?"—before I could get myself out of earshot and sight, a process that seemed to take several ages.

ONE MORE EULOGY

—for Forrest Bartlett (1936-2011)

I'D ARRIVED A BIT LATE, and the lot at the church had filled up. So I parked in a spot by the shady lawyer's office, which was closed on a weekend afternoon.

By the time I ran in, the tributes had already started, rough and funny and tender all at once, just like the dead man himself. We heard words I suspect had never been heard in that sanctuary, and wouldn't be heard again, but without them, none of us—over two hundred strong—would have found the hour right and true.

Our old friend died in the house where he'd been born. He logged, he farmed, and whenever he could, he went hunting. The reminiscences tended to dwell on all that. *One of a dying breed:* the phrase kept repeating itself, as if it had been invented for him. Nowadays the breed's descendants have generally left the farm, but they haven't found a better thing to take its place. Most live in trailers or shabby apartments, and the only hunting they do is for work, which has lately been scarce.

Even if I hadn't watched some tough people cry that day, I'd have cried on my own, just as I'd have laughed even without hearing others' laughter, or the jokes told aloud by an arty-looking woman about how she, a Vegan, for the love of God, could have loved him so.

"Sure, he could get worked up," said his friend John the blacksmith. *"He might take a poke at you."* But John reminded us as well that he'd be there if you called him for help *with your cow or your wood or your heart.* The dead man didn't want preachers at his burial, so it was the blacksmith who spoke the eulogy, a word whose meaning, he admitted, he'd had to look up: "A formal speech in praise of someone who's died."

I wouldn't have called John's eulogy formal, merely perfect. Cow or wood or heart indeed. Furthermore, what it said was all true. Try making the same claim for that lawyer, for the politicians, for the smug professors.

John ended the service with "After Apple-Picking" by Robert Frost, partly because another of our late friend's callings was that of cider-maker. Truth is, he did more or less whatever he needed to do.

Where I'd parked was not, after all, the lot for the shady lawyer but for the tenants who lived above the next-door laundromat. A tattooed woman with a basket of wet clothing, her voice rough with smoke, got all worked up because I'd taken her space. "I don't give a shit why you're here," she snarled. My temper might easily have flared; yet all I could find to say was, "I'm sorry. Jesus, I'm sorry."

COUNTY HOME:
AN IRAQUI SUITE, 2004

*—in mem. Robert Bagley,
and for the Reverend Ms. Susan Tarantino*

I. *Hex on the Vampire*

Months back, the preacher told me I should go and see him,
because our left-wing Christian sect requires "the ministry
of the people." So here I am to pick up Robert at the county
home, to speed with him in near absolute quiet to the truck
stop. We arrive, and he shuffles beside me, feeble, a brad-thin
arm hooked under mine, as we make our slow way through
the idling 18-wheelers in the lot, then into the unsmiling
company of their drivers, rough-hewn Québecois. This is
the first truck stop south of the lately terror-stricken, closely
guarded border.

Please God, I think, don't let me be a vampire, whatever
in my art may prompt me to be. I will force myself to be silent, letting the old guy order for himself, attending his artic-
ulations, the dark den of his mouth twisted by—no, I won't
tell you. I won't tell anyone, at least for now, what happened
to make him this way some years ago.

We eat, still unspeaking, and I don't wipe the egg from
his one and only necktie. No. The writer won't comment on
how Robert's doing as his trousers ride up his milk-blue shins

and he keeps on smiling. I'll tell you only that he may just be doing better than you or I: he'll take the world as it is. He's alone, he's dirt poor, he's ancient and lame, and is nonetheless a man who, unlike me too often, seems to understand the difference between acceptance and resignation.

I'm hungry. I order the "Big Rig Platter," steak and eggs, with bulky bread and the bottomless cup of good strong coffee. I mean to leave things at filling my healthy gut like a truck, forgetting about subject matter. He's taught me a thing or two, this shambles, this shell, though it's often a struggle to remember them. You see, I'm not doing good here. In the good-for-good department, Robert outpaces me, fueled by a meal of soft-scrambled eggs, crustless toast, and—it being a big day, in fact his birthday—tomato soup.

Robert's shirt is cross-buttoned, his trousers climb those shanks, his dank and slow-grown hair is harum-scarum.

Awkwardly, I pray, *Please God, don't let some literary effort of mine reflect on those crumpled shoulders, the head that lolls and allows the white, bowed neck to present its length, as if for my teeth.*

II. *Dated story*

On my way in, I see the two women whom I think of—without irony, I hope—as the Sleeping Beauties, small in their nineties to the cusp almost of infinity, and always resting, always utterly quiet, thus apparently peaceful. And peace is, after all, a rare thing of beauty.

A war's still on, and "Rumsfeld's 'Saddened' By Criticism of Iraq Policy." So says this morning's headline above the syndicated article in our small, local newspaper.

When I get to Frenchy's room, I notice his daughter has woven a handsome Boston Red Sox blanket with "For Daddy" stitched at the top. A small, crocheted stocking shows on every door in the hall. It's just before Christmas.

Frenchy was born in 1918, which was until now the last year the Sox were World Series champions. It'll be a good holiday, then. Fact is, he's not saddened. Not at all. Fact is, he tells me, he's happy as a bull with a heifer. Despite my poor ears and his spectral voice, I hear and I laugh.

One of my older neighbors recalls Frenchy's gas station in the 1950s, which he'd bought and run for a long spell because even then Vermont's family hill farms were in trouble. She tells me Frenchy was a very nice man.

Frenchy *is* a very nice man, and not all that ill; he's just old, is all. He jokes that when he was a boy, "That Big Dipper wa'n't nothin' but a little cup." He laughs again, a sound like gentle wind among reeds on the river, as I used to hear it from blinds when the duck hunting was a lot better. I laugh again myself, even if I'm a touch wistful. I was a fitter, younger man when I hunted those ducks, so I get to thinking of time's velocity.

As for Mr. Secretary, he claims that time is precisely the issue, not will, and in another context I'd agree, because true enough, time is a killer. But Rummy isn't talking of philosophy but of making armor plating for our soldiers' Humvees, which his department could not, apparently, manage to provide before the US invasion.

He has advised our troops that "you go to war with the army you have and not with the one you may wish you had," no matter it seems clear as death to an ignorant man like me that he and his cronies had all the time in the world in which to plan their precious assault. Frenchy doesn't have that kind of time; but then, as far as I know, he bears no responsibility for a single death, either.

"By God we did it!" Frenchy calls out loud, or as loud as he can, while I'm leaving. You might think he had driven in runs himself, or pitched scoreless innings, or turned double plays, and so had helped to whip the hated foes. But it's just the ironist in me that notes such a thing, and I've become ironic only because so many people's claims are—excuse me—bullshit, whereas Frenchy's joy is real, I think, and I know I am right, and his joy is not petty, because there's no such thing as a petty joy in the world.

III. *Unspent*

There's been more snow in March alone than there was all the rest of the winter, so I'm guarding against the ice that forms beneath its cover after rain or thaw swells brooks and then a freeze drops in to sheet the surface over. In time, the brooks subside, the water drops, the drum-ice turns into a trap.

"Not me, goddamn you!" I shout into still air. I probe with a ski pole. That ice is thin as a dollar, I suddenly think, and having thought it, I go on to think of old Reed at the home.

Reed said last week he had unspent cash in his wallet. He showed me a bill so worn you could scarcely make out the figures on the bills. "Older'n God," he sighed. So I took him down to the general store, because he'd been in no store for ages and had forgotten what it was like to visit one. A store! A store was all, for the love of God. And I've got nothing to do this Saturday afterwards but poke around with a pole and swear.

Today, the president told the public he was on a mission to change Social Security. *Reform.* That's the word he used. His plan would put all retirement accounts into the hands of Wall Street's brokers. The brokers love it. Now it's true enough, Reed's benefits can't pay for any care but what he gets in his tiny room at the county home, which not that long ago was known as The Residence for the Poor, but will Wall Street help that? I have my doubts. By now the home's name has been softened, and its staff's damned good, as good anyhow as it can be under the circumstances. A decent staff is not the point, however.

The only stock Reed's ever gotten over the counter is his stock of drugs, whose manufacturers are likewise fond of so-called reform. Most of the time, the pharmaceuticals keep Reed from hitting bottom with seizures. I mutter and keep right at my probing. I don't want to sink into some neck-deep pit with a crash. Whenever I find a patch of drum-ice I just bash the living hell out of it, then hop across the brook or ditch as I still can do, praise God.

In that general store I figured I should let Reed spend his money, because, just for a change, he wanted to buy whatever he could himself. He fished up two of those pale bucks for doughnuts and tea.

I'm out here by myself for now. Not for good. For now. *A person needs some dignity,* I think, but I'm standing alone in woods, where that issue isn't an issue, where only ravens and rodents hear me curse and flail, and wish out loud I could see the reformers spend one year at making bread, loaf after loaf, as Reed kept doing for forty years and more, so that his hands are forever locked in a curl, as if he were still kneading dough.

Then those who rhapsodize on *an ownership society* would spend one week in the home, good staff or none, where Reed sits quietly waiting for somebody to join him in front of the lone TV, on whose screen the owners keep prosing away, their discourse full of high-sounding bromides. *Dignity. Responsibility. Freedom.* So on. Each day for Reed is like treading that dollar-thin ice. Each day is a day is a day is a day in the home. I crash my crude weapon against the goddamned ice until the croaking and chattering wild things scatter, as if I possessed not a pole but a gun.

IV. *6-9-9-1*

6 is for the number of strokes that left Joe what he is: one big stroke, then five of those little ones called by letters. I forget which letters, but one is *I*, for *incident*, as I recall.

You wouldn't think Joe's mouth could be so black, so hollow. I like to see him smile, and at the same time don't. You wouldn't think a back could be so bent, either. And yet, whenever I arrive, he straightens as best he can to present himself to me.

I've been with him this morning for a few minutes, which, I scold myself, aren't enough. Yet I keep on punching the code.

9 now. What else can I do, after all? He can't walk, he can't talk, it will have to be enough—won't it?—that I come to visit once a week and after only a while I return to this great metal door and punch the numbers, whose order he's not allowed to know, though he couldn't escape if he tried.

These short visits are all I offer Joe. He has no one else on earth. So am I a hero? You bet I'm not. Not at all, but he does notice me there, I believe. He's aware that I stand by him now and then to hear the Bingo numbers, say, and to help him put down his chips, gently slapping him on his back when he wins. Today he didn't win.

So I have walked down this Pine-Sol-and-urine-reeking hall and I'm punching these other numbers on the big, cold door. Oh, here I am again at my blessed *6-9-9-1*, I think, and although it can't be right, I feel I'm free at last.

I'm still only at the second *9*. I'm much younger than Joe but I'm slow with the code because my eyes don't do well in such low light. He was a roofer down in Concord and probably known by his full name there, not just Joe. I don't know the other name myself.

Joe and I are friends by now, to call it friendship, and you always want, of course, to help a friend or any fellow human as much as you can—except you can't. Or maybe you can but you don't know how. For instance, I have only held Joe's shriveled claw and shouted at him to nod if he needed anything and pointed to his shirt, shoe, toothbrush, and so on. He didn't nod. I didn't ask about the TV or radio because he can't quite hear them anyway, and his roommate is asleep. All he does is sleep. He won't be watching or listening to anything. At least Joe sits there waiting.

I push this last number, the *1*, which could stand for *I* too, I suppose, and once I touch it—*poof*—I'm gone.

OUR HEADS AGAINST THE WALLS

REGGIE BEGINS, "I didn't get in trouble every time I drank, but every time I got in trouble I was drinking." He and I sit on our folding chairs, ten inmates on theirs.

I like Reggie. I like his thinking. I even like his God and his prayers. I like his small herd of Morgan horses, whose coats come brilliantly alive when the sun hits them. I like how he talks about his wife. I like his wife.

On our way to the prison, we passed the farm of his childhood, where ancient cellar holes gape here and there in such woods as were spared when those hundred acres got developed and took on names of things that so-called development pushed away forever: Black Bear Road. Grouse Lane. Wood Duck Circle. It was already dark by the time we passed.

We'd agreed to come here to discuss a problem we both know a lot about. Most of these cons do too, though few will admit it. I only spent a few nights in the slammer myself, for disorderly conduct. I was drunk, of course, as I always seemed to be once upon a time, the same as Reggie, though he got locked up much more often and for much longer spells. He was a brawler, a scary one, if talk's to be believed.

But here he sits all peaceable, even while he recalls being teased as a child. He jokes that he was so wall-eyed in his school days that his tears ran down his shoulders, not his cheeks. "I got madder'n a hornet," he admits, "and I grew up a scrapper." He stayed that way until he said the first of the only two prayers he uses to this day: *God help me.* The other one's *Thank you.*

Reggie claims he knows what a miracle is: "It's getting what you need just when you need it most."

As soon as he was sprung, Reggie would find himself dragged back in, sick drunk and fighting furious. "I had to have enough to *call* it enough, see?"

I think I notice one inmate studying the floor and faintly nodding. But the other jailbirds have come for a break and some good behavior time. Reggie and I know that. You can't get blood from a stone. We know that too. What's the cliché? *Been there, done that.*

"Broke heads and puked and did things I can't imagine now. Like I stole a rope . . . and it had a cow hooked on it." Reggie chuckles; so do I; the prisoners don't. "No one done them things for me. You got to take some action, can't stay right there where you are."

He tries his silly slogan: "God don't steal parked cars."

A smirking felon speaks up. "I do," he says.

Now the inmates do laugh, and, in that small room, laughter feels like a relief.

WOMAN AND DOG

I'D FOUND HER THERE SEVERAL TIMES before when I came to hike. She made me curious, perhaps unforgivably so, the way she'd scuttle like some small animal behind the moldering cabin that marked the trailhead, or the gray barn abandoned in a field full of popple whips.

Or maybe it wasn't truly abandoned: someone always seemed to stock the barn's mow with the summer's hay, baled tight, no wilt or dampness. But the hay was the least of several enigmas there, the woman herself the most. She came to gather windfall apples, accompanied by a mongrel dog who looked to have a tumor, ovoid and flat, below his stub of tail.

How did they live? Where did they go when they left?

When I first came to climb that sugarloaf mountain for its splendid prospect of fall foliage, I tried to greet her on several mornings. She never replied, and I speculated that she might somehow have lost her power of speech.

Her grooved and toothless face, her hands, her jacket, mittens, cap and trousers were all weathered drab as camouflage. She'd scoot behind one of those buildings, and then, I figured, into the brush behind. That is, she behaved like prey, and that seemed motive enough for me to hunt her, despite what should have been my better instincts.

I'd push through hardhack, Joe-Pye, burdock, and berry canes, but would always end up frustrated and bloodied by thorns, an outcome that made me even more determined to root out the woman and her dog whenever I came again. The dog never seemed to bark. Maybe I'd try to sneak up on the two. For whatever uncanny reason, I could never find them otherwise after they flushed.

Why should I alarm such creatures? What exactly could I want of so luckless a pair that I'd waste those precious minutes when I might have been well up the mountain already?

This all went on so many years ago I can't remember how I justified such behavior. As I think back, it simply can't be justified. No, I'm ashamed to say, it was just that the challenge caught my fancy. Taking it up signified some mean propensity in me, no doubt, but I must have tried not to think about that.

Today I'm glad I always failed at unearthing those two. Perhaps the woman had trained her silent dog to disappear as deftly as she did, the way a rodent might flee weasel or hawk. When the mongrel bolted after his owner, his hideous growth, abraded red, was the one bright thing I'd see. Indeed, with every encounter, the view from the mountaintop struck me as duller than it once had been, or than it should be.

SAME OLD PATH

2010 SAW that dreadful Haitian earthquake, to which dear friends of ours lost a son, and in the same week a cherished former student of mine, only forty, collapsed of a heart attack in Savannah.

Here, two years later, my dogs appear to be sniffing some winter-killed animal ruin. I shout them off it. Spring, that cliché of regeneration, seems hard to envision.

Surf raked at a Georgia shoreline, hot wind clawed a Haitian mountain, but our own late winter remains almost perversely blue. I climb to stay fit as I can, choosing the same trails the wild game uses. I read tracks in the snow. Sometimes it's I who make them first, at other times the creatures.

I stop where a brook hums under ice. Life is good, I say; but my mind's a spiral, and I know better than to liken this blather of water to song. I stride long, not to break through.

How would *good* sound to the dead young men's parents or lovers?

It's as if I've chosen this path I'm on, but I know that any footed thing would have chosen the same. It's just the logical way to go. I have no special instinct.

For now it's a moose I'm studying. The size of its hooves might compare to a headstone's, I muse, then I stop in my tracks: no figure of speech stands up to desolation.

We're all just along for the ride, however long we persist in our movements. I'm holding on for dear life, though I'd thought to follow something, and thought I'd be followed by something.

A CHRISTIAN, 2005

ALTHOUGH WE WEREN'T OF THAT ORDER, David and I wanted to visit Agion Oros, holy site of the Eastern Orthodox Church. As the rickety bus crawled past the goats and skinny hamlets and roadside icons, we could now and then see Mt. Athos in the distance; but when we reached Ouranopoli, we were told the pilgrim boat would not be sailing today, the fabled wine-dark sea gone muddy and rough, even though at the ferry wharf the weather didn't seem like much. Small waves, small wind.

As passengers stood around, one put the touch on the sweet Albanian student we'd chatted with as we rode out from Thessaloniki: "Hey, foreign boy," he drawled in comfortable English, "you got a cigarette?"

Smiling, the young man proffered his pack, from which he let the stranger cadge not one but several smokes, after which the moocher, without even a nod of thanks, strolled off twenty yards or so and began animated conversation with some slightly thuggish-looking companions. We told the Albanian boy how generous he was, but he only shrugged: "They aren't gold, just cigarettes," he said, and smiled again.

Soon enough, the smoker returned. Shooting his eyes back and forth from David to me, he talked about living ten years in New York: "I'm glad that's over," he concluded. "You must be shaking like puppies back there. This terrorist business . . . you all must be scared shit."

We admitted things were different.

"It's because of that idiot Bush," the stranger went on. Though he growled, he seemed strangely delighted: "The Jewish lobby . . . He licks their asses. They run the whole damned world, the filthy bastards."

David and I were trapped there waiting, so we only looked away.

The Greek persisted: "Listen: I've been around, I know. I lived a long time in New York. Kike-town."

The kind Albanian, trying to help us, maybe to head off something ugly, and having learned I was a poet, began to speak of Allen Ginsberg, whose work he'd read in the original and liked.

"Ginsberg?" asked the smoker, looking around the room at the Pilgrim Center, as if the late author might be found here in this company of visitors and monks. "America, go fuck yourself with your atom bomb!" he recited, too loudly. Heads turned. He grinned. "Oh, that Ginsberg! A personality."

I said I'd known him slightly, and he was that indeed.

"We should kill some Turks," the man muttered, out of thin air. "Take our beloved cities back. Butchers, they are." I half expected him to quote Nazim Hikmet.

Then he left at a trot to eastward, as if quick-marching, exactly, toward Turkey before he came back for the boat, which would, if the weather calmed, take pilgrims like him to a place where it's claimed a savior has been worshiped almost from the dawn of Christian times—Jesus, son of the God *Who maketh the lion to lie down with the lamb.*

What is the Son of Man that thou visitest him? I rolled that one over in mind too. Psalm 8. It's a favorite of mine.

MICKEY

RYDER, ONE OF THE WRANGLERS, told us what Mickey had done, and I plain *knew* that if the gun and the whiskey jug hadn't stood in the cabin at the same time then poor Mickey would probably not be graveyard dead.

This was our first day back in badlands Montana, an annual retreat I take every year with my old friend Peter; I have no better partner. It's almost comical: he and I are just tree-hugging liberals from the perfidious east in the eyes of ranchers and hands, yet we've all turned out to be friends after these many years. Ryder must have noticed that the two of us were fighting back tears, or I know I was, but I didn't really care if I looked like a sap.

It had been a Sunday when Mickey announced he was off to take a nap after lunch. But, along toward dinner, he still hadn't come back from his trailer, so Jamie went out to call him in. "Soon's I saw the blood, though" he told us, "I called the sheriff instead."

Mickey had been a POW in Vietnam, and facing time for a third DUI, he wrote: "I'm all through with cages." He'd seen time harder than I can imagine. Still, he wouldn't have blown his own head off if not for the jug. I know that much in my heart. When you're where Mickey was, you don't decide: *either* bullet or bottle. Both are part of the deal, lacking a miracle.

By now he had worked at that same spread for ages. So it was surprising that Peter and I didn't know of the Vietnam ordeal. But then no one ever mentioned it, not Mickey, not his bosses and the other cowboys. Like anyone else, he joked and chatted at mealtimes. He was friendly enough, even if he did seem to keep to himself more than those other hands.

He was an ace at puzzles, above all crosswords. One evening he shocked Peter and me as we worked together on a clue: upper bodies. Mickey looked out the window and muttered, "torsi."

"It was a year in a glue factory taught me," he explained. "It took three hours for a batch to set up, and all I had to do while I waited on it was stir that mess now and again. In-between I done crosswords."

There's a strange beauty to those high plains, hardscrabble as they are, especially under that blue-dawn light of thin prairie air. Maybe beauty helped us a little to deal with the matter. But for all that, whenever I picked up a bird that one of us had shot, it wasn't the furnacey plumage of a rooster pheasant or the pale lilac iridescence above a Hungarian partridge's tail that I contemplated. It was jail. Not the hand-wrought one that Mickey had been in, and would have been in later; I thought of the one that lets you go on walking around, but blinds you to the possibilities you might find, at least now and then, in a different frame of mind. Some people stay caged there until it's the moment to live or die, period, and they live. Life stays a puzzle, to be sure, no matter. Some don't live.

After the dog fetched, the warm birds went wry-necked. I kept hunting, but for one of the few times ever, I hated the blood, and by day's end, hated the very sun as I watched it descend in steely bars, and even hated those lovely, unsympathetic stars.

TOWARDS EASTER, 2008:
EYE ON THE SPARROW

IT'S TINY, almost an anti-weight. If the wind blew it off my palm I might not even notice. Dashing against a window, the bird fell onto some logs I'd stacked, or rather heaped. I'd loaded the wood more neatly in the shed but hauled a cart-load onto the porch and left it in a jumble, which somehow reminded me that my life too often lacked grace.

It wasn't any gale that killed the bird, but misprision. The sparrow dreamed its path clear through what turned out to be double-pane glass.

My oldest daughter had given birth to twins the very day before, and I'd been thinking of them of course when I saw the bird. We were entering a hopeful season. I wanted to imagine new beginnings, rather, for instance, than pondering the self-styled Christian Warriors I'd heard about lately, devoted to killing police, to launching Armageddon. They claimed these were the days of the Antichrist, and I could almost agree—for other reasons from theirs. *Thou shalt not murder* is among the Commandments, I'd have reminded the warriors, all nine of whom lived in Detroit, a place near-hellish in this near-depression.

Days are bad worldwide, though gospel says God's eye takes in the smallest sparrow. Vile hooligans among us storm over having a president who's not white, but we're all human, and none of us saved, and—as the old Greek said—it might have been best if we'd never been born.

And yet to imagine a world devoid of hope and love is too easy, too lazy. Outside the odors of spring flew in on wind: damp mulch, old ice, wet mud and sap. The sugar-makers hoped for a few more gallons, I hoped for a few more years, so I could stay with the little children.

I opened the stove and swept the bird in.

JAKE IN CIRCLES

—for Jordan and Britta

OUR SON AND HIS GIRLFRIEND were visiting. They had a dog back then, who, after he fought to his feet, would start moving around our kitchen, always counter-clockwise. The vet had referred to his ailment as *intracranial massing*, no doubt thinking the term would strike a tone less hopeless than *brain tumor*.

We didn't hear any quickness of breath or whining as Jake pursued his circles. You'd have thought him sound if you'd seen him. He showed good flesh, and his eyes were clear. Too bad in a way. If he'd been in obvious pain, his young owners might have found it easier to end it all. But who knows? Children for them were something in the future, so small wonder they clung hard to Jake, the first pet they'd had together. I remember that hefty son as a small, tow-headed boy, no less sweet and kind in childhood than he was as he watched his pet whirl, than he is as I write this down.

Jake, the people at the pound had surmised, was part yellow Labrador and part Shar-Pei, with tiny ears and a tongue as black as death. Odors of cooking, even the least, still caused that tongue to show. All of us there—mother, father, sisters—observed him helplessly.

Even though, right off, I felt a charge of self-distaste at finding some poetic association to render what we all observed, I somehow thought of a random morning in the May preceding, when I'd stepped outdoors into a shower of florets drifting in their thousands from every nearby maple. They fell in graceful circles to the ground.

That handsome young man and that pretty young woman have married since the morning when their dog walked round and round, and the one when those seeds dropped in their own rounds from the canopy. Needless to say, after striking the earth, at length they would rise from the earth and grow.

MICAH WEEPING, 1983

THREE DECADES BACK, the Vietnam War seemed well over for many of us. On Memorial, or Decoration Day, as our small town's elders still said, I watched Big Micah the plumber. There he stood, weeping while McClure's All-Student Band played taps on the village common. The flag was lowered to half-staff.

I was young then, yes, but not so damned young that I shouldn't have known *something*. After all, one of my best college friends, a roommate, in fact, had been blown to pieces out there almost twenty years back.

To be sure, his death was a big part of what got me going in the nonstop '60s protest happening. I'll tell you what, we sure knew how to party. No, we couldn't have found the enemy nation on a map, so I'll tell you something else: we were full of crap in a lot of ways.

We're all in our seventies now—those who remain, that is. I look back at myself in '83, and I cringe. I should have been better tuned in by then as I spied on Micah. A Korea veteran, he stood there crying in public, the tears all lost within his chins. I silently jeered him for a useless, fat boozer, spilling useless, fat boozer's tears.

I was half afraid the poor slob would bust his trousers with all his girth as his crying shook it, or the seams blow out of his army-issue shirt. There was so much else in the world I could have imagined, but then again, no one had shot at me,

I hadn't seen anyone bleed to death, so I thought Micah just looked loopy in fatigues and a cap that seemed to be melting down his head, like snow from a roof.

At the bandstand, somebody was mouthing the usual boilerplate about honor and duty. I stood on the grass, in love with my own cynicism.

It wouldn't be long before Micah drank his pancreas away. Gunfire hadn't, but liquor knew how to kill him. And now his grandson, just back from Iraq, is about the same as the old man, though more reclusive. The boy's cousin, who went to school with my oldest son, tells me Little Micah just stays in his room, drinking and brooding.

I wish Big Micah could show up again today. I might have other, better things to say, if only to myself, including, minus any irony, his name.

THE USUAL WAY

OUR BUS STREAKS BULLET-FAST by the soaring Crowne Plaza Hotel and the sundry Hartford insurance companies' towers, where, for all I know, millions of dollars are made and lost in a day. I don't care. I'm searching for something else as I cross Connecticut toward New York City to greet my daughter's newborn twins.

From my perspective, we should think of a child as constituting the highest form that spirit can know, and I'm headed south to witness such spirit, twofold!

All high-sounding enough, but I'm still petty, comparing myself to the unmannerly young couple bellowing laughter in the seat behind me, perhaps at the latest YouTube clip. What can their futures hold?

But what, after all, of my own? And why do I judge them, or that portly man, say, who fetches spreadsheets and memos from an outsized briefcase and frantically paws through them?

We're all after something.

There's WiFi on the bus. I get news from far distant friends and respond. This, I understand, is our world: disembodied connections, steel and carbon, thousands on thousands of roaring engines, whirling electrons.

I need to come to grips with my lifelong defect: believing my thoughts alone are true and proper, that my stories are true and definitive. Through headphones I hear an Art Blakey

CD. I say I seek something higher, yet I hear my music on disc, and material scalpels freed my granddaughter painful hours after her brother arrived in the usual way.

And this road I travel is material culture too. I labor a moment over such a recognition, but then, despite myself, I tritely sigh over Good Old Days and ruinous change. That's my own usual way.

A driver creeps past us, clinging like death to the wheel of her gargantuan sport utility vehicle. Her early-teenaged boy sits oblivious beside her, jabbing at a keyboard. I've seen those games, and know what's in them: automobiles and buses and towers in flames on the screen. The kid chews his lip, his eyes wide open, though not to the lovely green planet ablaze and spinning around him.

Plump, smut-darkened raindrops start to patter, laced with poisons that should scare us stiff. I hear the bus's wipers, each long as an arm, beating a sluggish tempo, as if there remained all the time in the world for us riders to salvage things we've been neglecting, to true our thoughts and behavior, to leave our grandchildren something.

HOW THEY WAVED

I RECALL GEORGE'S HAND on the horizontal, high over his wrecker's steering wheel, palm down. He'd make the hand swoop and wobble, like a wind-tossed bird. It didn't matter that, driving, I could barely see his fingers. I knew they showed the crankcase oil and axle grease that came with his mechanic's trade. How many electrical glitches and engine sputters and mud-mired cars did he help me with?

I'd wave back.

I remember another vanished friend as well. There was never a soul on earth so laconic as Bill, but that hardly meant he wasn't good-hearted. An understated man, not dour, he always grinned, however subtly. He would lazily raise a hand, or rather the very tip of its index. As he passed, I thought how, Christmas tree farmer that he was, his hands always smelled of resin and open air.

I'd wave back.

The sign on Harry's lawn boasted that he could "Fix Or Repair Most Anything." Only he, perhaps, understood the exact distinction between fixing something and repairing it, though, having brought everything to his door over many years, from goose-plucker to vacuum cleaner to push mower in need of sharpening, I fancied I knew which was which too.

No matter the season, Harry would pump his fist out the open window of his trail-worn International Scout, as if he were pulling on some church's bell-cord. That pumping always brought to mind other hand gestures that he made whenever he spoke his most considered thoughts out loud. They were good thoughts as a rule.

I'd wave back.

They'd salute me, I'd salute them. That was another time, in another sort of New Hampshire. It's been decades now since my family moved here to Vermont, just across the river.

It's the first day of January, another year waving good-bye to its predecessors, just as I did those three good men, all gone now, an age ago.

SHORT SAD STORY

As he pushed open the door of room 116 at the Longhorn Motel, I noticed the stranger's befuddled grin. "Oh, this is—" he mumbled, trailing off, backing out. I had hours to wait before I flew back east from Denver, so, seated at a chipped Formica table, I'd been trying, with small success, to rough out a piece of writing. As if it would help my efforts, I locked the door against further distractions, even benign ones like this petty mistake.

A few minutes later, however, the knob began to rattle. I slid the bolt. "What's the matter?" I snapped when I saw the same man standing there. "Can't you read numbers? *One-One-Six.* That's me, not you." The other didn't appear to hear. He leaned against the door with one shoulder, cradling an ill-sorted bunch of clothes in both hands.

"Get the hell out of here!" I snapped, because he started directly to lean against *me.* The interloper was a younger but smaller man than I. Putting my forearms against his chest, I shoved him hard, so that he fell outside onto the lot's asphalt, a plaid pajama top flying one way, a gravy-stained shirt the other, and a sock landing over both eyes like a flimsy blindfold. Even masked, his face wore that silly smile. It might have been a comical sight otherwise. I relocked my door.

My writing continued to go nowhere at all, so, in spite of the time gaping before me, I decided to repack my own clothes. Then I shaved, though I really didn't need to. I couldn't make those minor chores last long, however, and soon I headed for the lobby to grab a cup of coffee from the motel's vending machine. On my way, I spotted the erratic fellow once more. He was up on his feet at the very spot where I'd bowled him over, his odd bundle of garments re-gathered, the smile still showing, though not directed at anyone or anything in particular, least of all at the one who'd shoved him.

I asked the desk clerk. "What the hell's the story with that guy?"

"Seems like he's lost," the clerk answered. "I gave him the key to room 124, but he keeps tellin' me he needs to get into 116."

"My room," I mused, obviously.

"I figure he's drunk as a skunk," the clerk snarled, turning brusquely back to his affairs.

I went out for breakfast, dawdling for more than an hour over my meal and small talk with the sweet old waitress at a beanery called The Country Fare. When I returned to the Longhorn, I found the showroom-clean, white Ford 150 still parked in front of 116, but its owner was nowhere to be seen. I stepped into the motel lobby again.

"What became of our friend?" I asked. The clerk said he'd found him in some other room, not 116 but not 124 either, the room he'd been assigned. Apparently, all he could say was, "I'm waiting for my daughter."

In the end, not knowing what else to do, the clerk had called the police. In due course, the cops summoned the EMTs.

I don't know what happened after that, because I left for my flight, much earlier than I needed to. On the way to the airport in the rental car, seated by the gate, airborne, and all through the long drive northward to Vermont after touch-down, I couldn't help feeling rotten about having heaved that guy onto his backside. I understood why guilt might bother me as it did; but I couldn't quite sort out the other ways I felt. I tried to console myself, of course. How, after all, could I have known that the trespasser was not of sound mind?

Yet almost a year later, I still sense that same mix of guilt and whatever else may be. If anything, my trouble of spirit has strengthened, broadened, as if it may last me lifelong. Perhaps at least I can write about it. Maybe I *have* always written about it in some vague way. Whatever it is.

I remember arriving at our house that night, dog-tired in body and heart, and, right after supper with my wife, going up to bed; but a more powerful memory is of a dream I had some time toward dawn, in which that wonderful wife stood by me and the second of our three daughters before a bonfire we'd lit at the end of our woodlot road. A quiet bliss pervaded the vision, or rather a feeling like the peace that the apostle Paul describes, *which passeth all understanding.*

For a moment, still pretty much asleep, I guess, I arrived at the warming conclusion that such peace might actually remain in the world even after I left it, and that somehow it could be available to any person sufficiently needing it. Coming to, I felt desolate to recognize my fantasy as just that.

There had been times when I needed such peace for myself, and there would be other times to come. I knew as much. I hoped it would be accessible again, though I understood I couldn't simply will it into being.

I didn't think of the smiling man at the Longhorn right away, though shortly I realized I might have.

DARK CHORD

—remembering Jack Myers

SOME HOURS BEFORE I got on the road for here, I'd slipped the DVD, *Mingus in Europe*, into the player at home. There he was on bass, with Eric Dolphy on alto and bass clarinet, Jaki Byard on keyboard, Dannie Richmond, drums, Johnny Coles on trumpet, and Clifford Jordan, tenor.

They looked so young and strong. They were so gifted. But poor Dolphy died within months of that tour in '64 while I finished up my chaotic college years. I was surely no genius. I had not much to offer the world, compared; but here I still am.

Here happens to be a jetty by the Atlantic, along with a clutch of other friends and family. We've gathered to scatter the ashes of Jack, our dear poet friend, into the waves.

A pair of scoters skims quickly by while two young lovers embrace, the way young lovers are supposed to do on a beach, and I watch the moon rise full. All is perfect, it seems—except that Jack's not with us.

His absence may account for the sound, which has nothing, really, to do with the intricate magic of that Mingus sextet I listened to, nor with any line or stanza from Jack's mournful, witty, brilliant poems, nor is it the cry of sea birds. If Wagner didn't drive me almost mad, or maybe because he does, I'd say that the chord was a dark Wagnerian one. It washes over me the way surf does a rocky shore.

An aunt or cousin showed me a picture this morning: Jack at seventeen, right here in Winthrop, Massachusetts. He's sitting on a motorcycle, cocky and handsome, and it's oddly as though I somehow *hear* that photograph too. Jack sounds so young and strong. His engine rumbles while he banters in the Boston brogue he never lost.

A boyhood friend has a word or two to say as well, but he breaks down before he can finish.

"I'll miss him terribly," says our sweet friend Mark.

And terrible it'll be, yes. So when I hear the chord again it reminds me—as I fight for balance on these slippery rocks because I'm Jack's age exactly, damn it, older than those masters of jazz, vibrant, alive, holding forth in Europe back in a year when I was only 21: the chord reminds me—as I note the scoters winging back and the lovers walking under the moon, and I note the ocean breeze of good Jack's childhood, and think I could be noting all this idly, as believe me in this moment I'd love to do—the chord reminds me that *Something big has been shaping up for years and years and now you know, old man, it's for all of us here, including you.*

IT'S A BEAUTIFUL DAY

THERE'S WIND DOWNLAKE from the most brilliant quarter, north-northwest, but it's still gentle enough that the cumuli move slowly, grandly. In the water, low ridges and even jags of cloud show so sharp in reflection it looks as though they could cut your thumb.

It's latest summer, and the river salmon have grown fighting faces for October, when the spawn comes on. I can already see them, if I dream of standing on the bridge in the village: a thrash and spangle among the shallows, two males having at it below, until the weaker one resigns at last and fins out at an angle into the current to fade downstream.

On the west bank, the cedar waxwings will throng Mrs. Barton's mountain ashes, birds so preternaturally clean and well groomed I'll blink. I'll marvel at the berries, too, red as the reddest thing God made. The light will be the light of light off a waxwing's feathers. Once, even if I tried, I could not catch my breath for them, and even in waning Augusts like this, I'd have gazed in wonder along the lake or down the river or up into woods, where the feebler maples already show a subtle but eloquent flaring.

Below the canopy the sweet fern has started ineluctably to brown, and in the clearings, the hardhack to purple.

Yes, once I'd have gone half mad over such things, filled with a young man's urge, almost catastrophic, to *make* something of this sensory surfeit: this conifer tang in the northwester's air, cedar water red in the shallower coves, ospreys and eagles wheeling above, screams dropping loud on the densely wooded shores. But you can't bank any of that against your future.

Nor could anyone bank the feel of the smoothly grained ash paddle I grip, made by Kenny, who got good and shot up at as he stormed a beach in Norm, then came home and built himself a cabin deep inland from Big Lake. He stayed there until winter, and came back to run the store again, with never another word of that awful conflict. He ran the store well and long and with honor.

There was always, of course, the very water, a mere taste of which nearly drove me to frenzy. That craze of longing, that feeling of violent restlessness: it was at best a bother, at worst an ache, a bad one. Yes, I thought, a man must get up, and do, and do, and do.

Do what? Do something. Save all this unsalvageable glory. I now know to do nothing, because nothing can be done.

Yet what of the double rainbow I saw that time above the dam, for instance, or the otters that played tag with me as I paddled another lake with my wife, the way they barked at us now and again but never, it seemed, menacingly?

What of the sun, which always felt warm as a brick on my back while I plied the canoe? I recall those redtails, two-three-four-five—good God, it was six!—who would not be flushed from the lamb deer's carcass at the old Todd Farm one late fall, but hunched their collective shoulders, almost catlike, and hissed at me until I turned back up the tote road.

There's nothing I need to accomplish anymore, if ever there was. It's a beautiful day, and I'll just drift the near shores, have lunch at noon, then take a nap on a beach somewhere. I'm so much saner than once, and grateful for that. It's better. It's better. It's better. It's better to want so much less and hurt so much less. I'm calm as I watch the wind.

And yet and yet and yet and yet

The Beast
in the
Jungle

USA

IT'S THE SIXTH OF JANUARY, Epiphany, all of us creeping along in our cars, because there's this awful "mixed precipitation." We're creeping, that is, except for the odd fool in his immense, fuel-sucking SUV, which he, precisely like a fool, thinks can go anywhere and at any speed.

Everyone else is moving so slowly that I can take my eyes off the road now and then; I consider the sleet-and-grime-smeared Toyota Camry just in front of me, and even through that slurry can read its bumper stickers.

Talk about mixed! "VIRGINIA IS FOR LOVERS" is prominent; to the left, it's "TAKE VERMONT FORWARD," and over one more position, "SUPPORT OUR SOLDIERS," and finally, above the tailpipe, "STATE TROOPERS PROTECT AND SERVE."

I'm fairly sure the driver is female, though it's hard to see. In any case, the person at the wheel has been to Virginia, and seems to have experienced some sort of romance there, maybe in the Blue Ridge Mountains, which are lovely, like the ones around us here, though I scarcely see them either, because of the mix. I've been to the Blue Ridge myself. Those are really the very same mountains as these invisible ones. They just lie farther south, and show more broadleaf woods.

But I digress. My message is mixed (the word seems inevitable), whatever that message may be, for it seems as unclear as this weather, unclear as that driver's sprawled mottoes. But TAKE VERMONT FORWARD is surely an answer to TAKE BACK

VERMONT, which began to appear on a few yard signs way back in the day when our Supreme Court sanctioned gay civil unions in this beautiful little green state, and they're still displayed in a few scattered places now that actual marriage, thanks to an act of the legislature, is legal for the gay population. I conclude, then, that the driver, if not herself a lesbian, is large-hearted enough, God bless her, to think the Court did right back then, that state government has done right since. I think so too. I'm for love and tolerance.

SUPPORT OUR SOLDIERS? Well, I'm for that too, although I think the optimal support would be to bring those boys and girls back home, one and all, because, as John Kerry years ago asked, "Who wants to be the last to die for a mistake?" And what else was that mess in Iraq? What is it to this day? What's going on in Afghanistan? If that driver's for tolerance and love like me, surely she can't be cheerleading for war as well, can she?

Then there's STATE TROOPERS PROTECT AND SERVE. Well, yes, I believe they do. What do you think I am, some wild-ass dreamer who believes the world's a fairy tale? My late brother-in-law was a cop. He did and witnessed stuff so you and I didn't have to. I'm not ashamed to say I prayed for him every day to the end, and still do, as I pray for the troops.

I'm getting more and more scattered—not a good thing when the driving's bad—because I'm thinking all at once about love, tolerance, war, authority, and now God.

I *am*, however, one of those liberals who claimed a decade ago that he'd move to Canada if that villain and fool George W. Bush were re-elected. And yet I'm still here, though I do respect and admire our neighbor to the north, and even know a little about her, unlike most Americans, who seem to believe "We're Number One," no matter so many of us don't know a lonely fact about anyplace else on the planet.

My wife and I have experienced romance in Canada, as in Virginia. But yes, we're still here in the land of opportunity—and of war and authority, and at its best, of love and tolerance. We stay here because there needs to be, for random example, the "Tunbridge, Vermont World's Fair," where carnies, all sinew and smoke, flirt with local girls, and oxen in the stock barns loom so huge your jaw drops, and the odor of sweet dirty grease rises from the littered junk-food tents.

Like Epiphany, the Fair only happens once a year, same as Town Meeting, at which our neighbor Tink feels free, even if he never finished eighth grade, to tell the smart folks to go pound sand.

Oh, USA! My great big free, my all-mixed-up, my stupid, beloved, friendly home!

I LISTEN TO SOME BLUES

On my stereo player, Koko Taylor claims she can stop the lightning with just the palm of her hand, talk trash back at the Devil, make him crawl around in the sand.

But Koko's verse is just rhetoric, and mine surely the same. It's what she and I do. We may make lyrics, but when all is said and done, whether we do that or dig a ditch or shout satisfaction with some balance sheet, too many of us behave as if big talk will pull us through.

At four years old in nursery school, I was briefly king of a playground, even if the way I came to my kingdom involved corruption: I flat-out lied to my classmates, and they somehow believed my story that I'd seen a bee fly into the playhouse there, and had gone inside to stomp it into the dirt.

I just wanted to look brave. What manchild doesn't? Strangely, fortunately, no one asked me to display the minuscule remains of my kill.

That's a pretty small episode for me to focus on as a key to my whole character. Perhaps I make such a claim only because I need a proper plot. It really doesn't matter anyhow, because whatever the truth may be in that instance, it's still a fact that whenever I've played lordly wise, say, to my children, or run for local public office, or voiced my judgment on something or someone; whenever I've thought my opinion an enlightenment, and so a service, I've felt compromised, as well I should, given the skewed commentary that's involved.

Since one old day on a playground, the years have arrived and gone in a crowd, skittish as ponies. Once they seemed specks in the distance, then suddenly they were here at the fence, and as suddenly away again in a cloud of sand, if there can be such a thing.

And here I am after all, scarcely one to terrify the Devil. I just chatter and sing. Or I hold out my hands, as if I could keep things gathered within them, especially those years. Like others, I posture, I take my little stands. We all croon or purr or bawl or opine, but as we move along, each of us at some point will fall, metaphorically, down in the sand. We'll fall silent there and crawl, which may just be as it should be.

SMITTY'S NOT RIGHT

—remembering A.K.

SOMETIMES HE'S ISAIAH, sometimes Elijah, or even Jesus, though no one would see a prophet—much less a divinity—in Smitty, back on probation, rumpled and stinking. His lank hair's dyed some indescribable shade of blond. His lips clamp a roll-your-own smoke gone cold.

I'm a coward. I stay as quiet as a mouse, no matter I ought to laugh at, if only to save myself, and to shut him up. The man's not right, of course. If there's an Almighty, he'd hardly hand over the world to a wreck who has so completely used up mind and body with drugs and booze.

And the Supreme Being would surely have better strategies than conniving with Boeing. That's the latest vision: in a dream, a flight attendant led Smitty to a 747's emergency row. The emergency, it seems, was cosmic, and he the one elected to deal with it. The stewardess somehow knew that. She left him to work his power.

I'm a coward, so no, I don't scoff out loud; still, it's as if Smitty hears my thinking. With a sigh, he patiently re-explains what's what in God's world.

"Jesus," he begins, "was *tekton* to the Greeks." Lord, I think, what Greek on earth does this man have? No matter: he claims that a *tekton* was lowlier still than the carpenter Smitty now and then was himself—in the increasingly distant past. He thinks of himself as blessed *tekton*, though he

98

hasn't swung a hammer for an age, or done much of anything else to earn an income.

I'd like to point out to him that at least Jesus had a job., but I know Smitty would insist his real work's assigned from on high. He always does that, citing Scripture, which admittedly, he knows better than I do, to prove his argument.

I want to grab his shirtfront and say to his face, "Before you start saving the world, maybe you could get yourself straight." How many stints in jail for possession or minor peddling of drugs will it take? How many DUIs? "Don't worry about us mortals," I'd tell him. I don't say a thing, though.

He reads me anyhow: "I've fucked up before, I'll grant it." But now he claims he'll stay clean as the saints because he bears such awful responsibility, as his dream made clear. From the 747 he foresaw the awful radioactive cloud that in time will rise above the very town where he and I live, a hamlet so tiny you'd wonder why even Smitty in manic fugue or blackout drunk would single it out as a place for the Apocalypse.

I summon some guts and ask him about that. He darkens, scowls, and reminds me that what in my pride I call reason has nothing to do with eternal truth—and that will be the only part of his raving I accept entirely.

Smitty says he knows how my mind works. He knows I think his dream arrived while he slept. But it was holy revelation, and he received it wide awake. He was bodily lifted from the same scuffed plastic chair on which he's sitting now. We're on opposite sides of his unsteady kitchen table, where he came to roll that spit-stained cigarette. The tabletop sags with fat wacky tracts.

Assumed out of the chair and into that roaring jumbo jet, he had a view from Alpha to Omega. As always, I'm surprised by how easily and abruptly he can break out of jailbird slang into high oratory. "I was given," he intones, "to speak a word and set this earth on fire, or to keep my own counsel." Humanity's fate was up to him. Of course, it still is. Of course.

Then a light came upon him and he knew he must keep the sacred airplane flying, even though it was crowded with one vile sinner after another, from cockpit to tail. I was of their company, strapped in there just behind him in all his glory. He decided to keep me safe from hell, although I'd so often attacked him.

Attacked? That's the word he used. Yet all I've ever sought was to help him get clean and sober. Not that I'm any sort of savior. All I can rely on is my own crazy history as an addict, which therefore must be related to his, at least obliquely.

But is it? On my worst day prior to recovery, I wasn't as fucked-up as Smitty. Smitty's not right. I've had my own delusions, and probably still do, but his life and world are miles beyond me.

Still he says it again: "I have saved you—for now."

THE BEAST IN THE JUNGLE

What could the thing that was to happen to him be,
after all, but just this thing that had begun to happen?

—HENRY JAMES

THROUGH HOW MANY PREDAWN HOURS, my friend Bill
may wonder, must he lie awake with all these envies and re-
sentments intact before it happens: that glorious, long await-
ed moment when things at last will go *his* way?

Beside him in bed, the tranquil breathing of his beau-
teous wife once matched their long-gone children's respi-
rations down the hall. Bill remembered moments like that
in my presence a while back. He'd had a drink or two. One
more, and he remembered the owls' refrains every autumn in
his surrounding woods, and from the clearings, what sounded like crickets in praise, and in springtime, peepers' trills
from around his pond. (He's eloquent, even lyrical, when he
chooses.)

All these things should of course be more than mere
memories for him, but they seem not to be. His wife, though
aging like anyone else, remains a lovely woman, now as always.

Lately, Bill has turned more unsettled than ever, because
our mutual friend Jimmy, who's also Bill's longtime rival,
has finally gained notable fame as a painter, well paid for
each canvas he sells, and there are many. He's envious, too,

of another chum, Dan, whose physical condition is remarkable in a man of his, or really any, age.

When, oh, when will *he* get his due, and how? Bill asks such spoiled-brat questions aloud, chewing his lower lip. The whole routine embarrasses me; no, it irritates the hell out of me, if truth be known.

Now and then, as he's admitted, though my response is always guarded, he does think of certain high moments in his life, a life that, even without them, some would find attractive: that picnic, say, on a riverside beach, his red canoe belayed to a driftwood stump, flashy wood ducks dotting the reedy cove, and, strange and stunning, a fog that had withdrawn just as his little family launched.

All through their trip, however, a single strip of that fog hovered some fifty feet over the water, mapping the basin they paddled, with its oxbows and riffles. Bill loftily described it as a *lucent ribbon of mist*. It was shot with sunlight all morning, an Olympian ether, a sublimely gilded tracing, though these last are my own lofty terms.

Our athletic friend Dan can far outpace Bill up the mountains we all used to climb together. For my part, I take it slow, and Bill has to stop every so often these days in order to perform tiresome stretching exercises, as the long distance runner he's never been would do.

Renowned now, Jimmy the painter has no job to which he must travel; he can afford to go without any work that's unconnected to his art. Moreover, the insurance payoff after the trucker drove into and through the life of his poor son was a trove of redundant riches. Scarce compensation, as the ever melancholic Jimmy would tell anyone. He'd trade his every success.

As for Bill, when he drives to work, there seem always to be vultures above the road nowadays. He might observe the birds' grace as they wheel, but to him they look like conventional Hollywood metaphors for gloom.

He's so damned spry: that's all Bill ever considers when he thinks of Dan, with whom he once dashed to the tops of those hills, flushing birds in languid July from their cool, leafy arbors.

Bill has traveled a wider world since those days, to be sure. Once, as he sometimes recollects, he stood with that pretty wife and their children as they gaped into an alpine Swiss sky, split and spangled by fireworks that doubled themselves below in a green tarn. He should dwell on the likes of that.

He should recognize, say, that Dan had meant to be there in the Swiss Alps too, with a third fiancée, but before they could fly, she decided to break things off, blaming Dan's children, who'd never liked her. The cancellation of their engagement turned out a boon, because Dan later discovered the woman had secretly been a terrible pill addict. Still, Dan is famous for loneliness these days.

Bill insists his turn needs to come around. He yearns to rise, as bold and golden as that morning's mist on the river they paddled, or the sun at their bedroom window, pausing in its climb out of night's opacity into fulgent day.

BIG MUSQUASH STREAM

—for Christopher Matthews

TRUE TO ITS PASSAMAQUODDY NAME, the stream's alive
with muskrats, furtive little paddlers. The seemingly infinite
tract of slough that stretches from either bank shows domed
and gorgeous. Pickerelweed blooms on and on in the water, a
purplish-blue mass that almost matches the sky. The forecast
calls for storm a bit later, but I mean to push on, the sweeps of
my paddle narcotic. Lightning may threaten, but for now I'm
full of those sweet old delusions: that my way lies clear, that I
have nothing but time.

A cow moose grazes where Flipper Creek drops southerly
into the main branch. She wears a dangling pond-lily beard,
and she goggles at me, unfrightened, almost torpid, as insou-
ciant a creature as the world knows. I slightly bend the canoe
toward her, but she goes on blinking and chewing. I'm close
enough to see the gnats around her eyes.

Noontime. A flight of nighthawks has gathered above
the flow, untimely, not hunting but racing. I'm struck by
the beauty of their aerobatics, so pure and thoughtless, so
unencumbered.

I haven't explored this bog in some time, but surely it
can't have a thing in common with my gallant friend in the
Italian-speaking canton of Switzerland. He's all in a tangle,
living with pains of body and heart, both equally exotic to
him, and it might seem strange that he should enter my

thoughts on Musquash, were it not that I love the man and worry about him daily.

There's no soul for miles and miles—only muskrat, nighthawk, moose, and now some black ducks skimming insects from the backwash of a languorous eddy. The surface slick reflects the birds exactly, right down to their primary feathers, colored like the flowers and the sky. It's as though I'm asked to celebrate blue. I do, but there's more to be celebrated, despite my far-off friend's multiple sclerosis, so cruel and daunting, his crushing divorce. As for that love-grief, what could I tell him? That I'm glad I'm far past courtship myself?

I suppose I'm selfish, at least just now; I try to banish my own thoughts of the friend, wanting no distraction, let alone heart-heaviness, to mar this easy beauty as I slide over barely detectable waves. The small effort that my progress demands will be repaid: soon enough, I'll drift home on the faint current to my wife and love of over thirty years. That is, if I make it back to the launch ahead of that far thunder.

I'm sure I will. My constant returns make my absences worthwhile, as in the trite saying about hitting yourself on the head with a hammer: it feels so nice when you stop. But of course my trip hasn't hurt me, quite the contrary.

Despite myself, I think of my friend's quaint, ancient village, a speck on the map. Its precipitous hills make it hard for him to walk to the bus or the corner shop nowadays. It's always a challenge for me even to visit there. Some air of romance pervades the town, but its alleys twist into knots. You might hide that whole settlement in this vastness of bog, through which Big Musquash Stream so mazily wanders, though in the end there's only the one way out, and I know it.

HAVE I THOUGHT?

I SUSPECT THAT TO IMAGINE MY END is not the same as it will be to live out its crawling inevitability. But how can I truly know anything on that score? For all I can tell, death may be quick: perhaps a precipitous stroke as I lean to wipe hairs and dander specks from a cushion like this one, foiled yet again in my attempt to bar our dog's hopping onto it.

And yet the dog's comfort seems so much a part of my own that my effort to forbid such trespass is pretty faint-hearted. I can almost decode the scratches on the burgundy leather chair, glyphs the sweet retriever has carved into it as if to depict our common lives.

Or the ending could come as a heart attack like my father's. I have nothing but second-hand accounts, because I wasn't there to witness. I don't know whether that fills me with regret or relief. I have heard how awkwardly Dad fell. *I was not even twenty-four*: the phrase has repeated itself in mind for almost five decades since, ones through which I have continued to feel cheated. He was an excellent parent. I may drop like that. If I do, I can hear the commentary from those who'll be left: *He never knew what hit him*. It's a witless response to such collapse, but what would be more eloquent, really?

If the end does come slowly, perhaps it will feel less like catastrophe than like the slipping away of a love. Less a terror, then, than a grieving. My long-limbed wife appears in thought, and I taste the salt of my spontaneous weeping, no matter I can hear her as she readies herself upstairs, precisely, to walk the dog. I should go with her, but I'll stay home thinking. It's that sort of day.

The retriever, like all those preceding, belongs to the world of fragile earthly love, though less so than do our extended family's members. I picture the smiles of sons and daughters, grandsons and granddaughters, nieces, nephews, sisters, brothers. On and on. I picture one of this number, a two-year-old who loves to dance, his head bobbing, arms awhirl, feet high-stepping, and I simultaneously conjure the faces and voices of stalwart friends, ones who have stood by me for so much of my life, bearing with its elations and pains.

Through spring panels of rain, I notice an indigo bunting at the feeder. Its color stuns, and I rise to see the bird more clearly; but in that very instant I'm distracted by a she-turtle scrabbling down the drive, determined after burying her eggs to reach the dimpled pond. I go on to recall that wisp of snake in the turned garden, mere days ago, its sudden, lissome unwinding, which both unnerved and delighted me.

Have I thought right along that all I've been living was somehow eternal, the earth forever blooming, not shedding?

HOW DOES THAT
MAKE YOU FEEL?

AT A HARD CURVE ON Route 25, there's a tower with a birdhouse on top, the size of a steamer trunk and painted ice-blue. You'd think the birds might be scared off by that almost spectral color. The tower's legs are strung with a score or so more of birdhouses, like dangling Christmas bulbs, and the space inside the legs is full of still others, rough-piled there like loose flakes of hay.

What manner of people, I wondered, would decide to throw together this clutter, and why? Was it love of birds or birdhouses? Was *love* the word? I wanted the truth, but on the road to the vet's, even before I noticed the tower, I'd been a jumble of befuddled speculations.

Later, when he saw my hunting dog, the doctor said, "Bone cancer." Then he gave me narcotics to last him until he was gone. Could I have done something to save him? Who owns such power?

Back on the road again and feeling godforsaken, I wept and whimpered, though when I reflected, I recognized that I was musing on other things too, such as the fact that the dog didn't seem blue, or even ill, not to mention baffled like me. He just lay quietly in the car. Life was still life.

I drove on, still in tears, to visit my new grandchild: I pictured that peach-skinned girl, who was a miracle, and that someone like me could make her giggle and grin a greater one.

After some hours and back in my car, I remembered that the house beside the tower had had a sign in front of it, showing four block letters. Did they spell "LOVE"? I hoped so. I vowed to stop on my way home to examine the word and be sure, but I forgot my intention, lost in thoughts of dog and granddaughter both.

I sit here now and wonder by what earthly right I consider them strange, those purposeful birdhouse builders? Who am I to make such a judgment, I, whose very head seemed a cage of odd twitters, who feels nothing so firmly as uncertainty? One builds whatever one can, and however one will, I figure.

Home alone, my wife still at work, I imagine a whirl of flight: some of the creatures within it are drab, others brightly feathered. There are timid songbirds and ferocious raptors. They've all come back to roost in that family's yard. When they wing in by the score like this, I wish I could ask those people what a psychiatrist kept asking me years ago, before he'd write a script for pills to calm my nerves. *How does that make you feel?* He asked me and asked me. He asked me until I wanted to scream.

STORYTELLING AT THE RES

JOE HOPES HE'S A GOOD GUY NOW, but by jollies he wasn't a good one once. He says he even stole his own wife's hairlong jewelry to pay off a deal.

I have to smile: *hairlong*.

If you need a drink or drug, Joe continues, believe me, you'll take what you got to take. Go ahead and rob your buddies or, like he just said, even your very own folks.

Outside, cold rain is coming steadily, but it feels so warm indoors I'm afraid I'll doze, even though I'm not exactly sleepy, and Joe's story isn't boring. Not at all.

There was a time he worked a big saw, he says, and the whole while plastered. It's a wonder he never got himself or somebody wasted. There was a lot of days like that, and a lot in the joint too. Once he broke a white cop's arm with a tire iron. The cop and his pals didn't like that, you can bet.

Joe wears a raven feather in his hat, which he jokes about, telling how it shows he's gotten better, because it sure isn't no war bonnet. He tries to stay humble is what he's saying, just that one feather. He prays all his war days are done for.

"Anybody else got something?" he asks now. Everyone nods, but afterwards most just look shy and keep their mouths shut, except one guy in the room whose tribal name is See-Quickly, but people call him Jesse. He wears braids and has half an arm missing. He speaks up just enough to say he's glad he's out of prison. Again. I hear some scattered applause.

"They's a bunch of other people not here," Joe says, "some of them clean and sober for years. Then they disappear, and then you hear they're locked up, or else dead."

"What about you?" Joe asks, looking at me, one of the few white guys. "What you got?"

I try to say something, but it seems too hard to come up with anything but that I'm happy to be here, which I guess is true.

"No, no, don't nobody feel on the spot," Joe continues, shaking his head, which makes his jowls shake too. He's just a guy himself with some habits. "Like check out this gut—too many doughnuts."

But doughnuts don't make you lose it. I want to say that, because we are all in this place for being crazy once.

"You got something more, Jesse?" Joe asks. "Let's hear about it. Once you put stuff right out in the open, see, that helps you get it out of your system. You start in with that, then maybe you can get some healing."

Jesse says, "I don't even own no hat, never mind some bonnet. I ain't got shit."

Joe calls that God's will for now.

"So when I chopped off my arm at the mill, that was God working his ways on the res?" Jesse asks Joe, but he isn't pissed off; or anyhow he smiles.

Joe knows Jesse didn't mean anything bad. What happens, whatever it is, is what happens, he says. You might as well think there's a reason for it. I mean, check around here. Joe nods his head at everyone in his seat. I look down at the floor when his eyes get to me. "We're supposed to be where we're at. I just call that a God deal, even when our asses get throwed in stir, maybe even if we're killed. What do I know? I don't know what God is, except He ain't me."

I wonder if what he says next might not just be right, and it could include me: we all went to different schools together.

My trouble is, I want a story, and not just any story, but a knockout like Jesse's. The fact that I keep looking for that sort of thing means maybe I'm not so much better than I was when I was using after all. I have to be a lunatic or just a fool to have wishes like that, to believe I haven't been beat up enough to be interesting.

The blue tattoo on Jesse's stub shows only the top halves of letters; I can't make out the word they spell.

MY TIME MACHINE

I BELIEVED I WAS TOO HIP FOR WORDS and I wanted Susan to know it. I also wanted her to know—and anyone else who wanted to know—how well I knew my way around the Vanguard, how just for example I knew that odd little triangle table to the left of the stage was best for taking the music in, for taking in the presences.

That night the presence happened to be the great Charles Mingus.

Given the times, you might challenge my small preoccupations; but who, besides a few Quakers, had heard or cared about our "advisors" somewhere in Indochina?

It was said that Mingus had once fired his whole band right onstage, and it was common knowledge that he'd punched Jimmy Knepper, his own trombonist, right in the mouth. In fact, on the evening I summon, as his men performed "You Better Get It In Your Soul," his shouts from the stage seemed to burst more with rage than enthusiasm, or at least that's how I hear them now.

That night I made a mistake, which even today I ache to reel back, because to recall it is to rekindle a hopeless dream of some magical time machine that could erase my great embarrassment and get me back to Susan, back to that sort of evening (minus the famous blunder, of course), even if I know Susan and I were scarcely made for each other. I know, further, that my life could scarcely be better than it is with the woman of my later, better dreams.

Hell, Sue and I were just babies, whacked out on the booze and speed that would knock us both to our knees in the years that lay waiting. My machine would change much of what came with those coming decades, not just the disaster I launched when I started shouting too. I started shouting with Mingus.

It wouldn't be long after that everybody, it seemed, began to die overseas, and life all around us got angry, to put the matter mildly.

Mingus put nothing mildly. He cursed me back to my grandparents' generation, coming up with terms I can't or won't make myself repeat. That was such a hard voice, roaring as it did inside a room gone otherwise silent.

My friends and I would all be activists soon, for a while anyhow. We knew what we knew, which was rage, and we let everyone else know how we felt about things we found cruel or absurd. We made careless and furious love, to call it that.

When Mingus wound down his tirade, his band moved straight into "Gunslinging Bird."

NEVER

THE GENERIC PRINT OF A SEASCAPE HANGS crooked above the generic beige phone. There's misty rain out the window, and here inside, the smell of my own rank sweat on sheet and pillow. I may never get back home.

I lie here trying to devise some original way of feeling so ill, or of testifying to—something. It must be something important. It's just outside my ken as I lie here, trembling. I'll never find words to render it, and suddenly that seems so overwhelming I fear I'll drop cemetery dead. Of course, it's only this nasty, inconvenient illness that induces such grandiose thought. I don't even believe it as I think it.

Fever tortures my joints, sears my eyes and throat. I'll soon enough forget the physical sensations I'm having, here in this rented, nondescript room, along with my theatrical platitudes. I may even forget what seems like a tragedy now: precisely, that I'll never again find words adequate to my human situation, or anyone's. Ailing or well, I won't, I can't, I don't know how. For the moment, such thinking comes on me in so profoundly painful a way that I'm near despair.

It's only fever, I repeat, as it's doubtless fever that makes my recollections go antic: I remember our two younger daughters and me, all three of us supine in a hammock; we're seeing how many tunes we know, and singing all of them we're able. And then I recall a back pasture camp-out with the oldest son: I am all but hypnotized by the glitter of moon in his eyes. And next I conjure the airplane toy, mere nails and wood, I once made for the firstborn daughter, who seemed to think she beheld a masterpiece in my makeshift, crude contraption. In mind, the younger son, having caught his very first fish, sits staring, stunned.

Those children, understandably, have never grasped how much these moments have meant to me, and still do, no matter how frantically I might want to explain. I wish I could apologize for my parts in them, because they probably should have been better parts. Still I cling, and anxiously, to our history's remnants.

What if I lose even the remnants to some sudden seizure? What if I die?

I won't, not yet, but—febrile, and so achingly far away from my longed-for home, from my mate and confidante of these many years, from all I crave—I imagine how people may crawl toward their graves in useless, ineloquent tears, having never told a soul they treasure the things they burn to tell.

I whisper it: "Never."

Disconsolate, hoarse, I breathe it over and over in some dingy chain motel, *never, never, never,* though I'm sure I do so only because I'm sick.

RECOVERY ROOM

I HAVE LOVED THE WOMAN on that tilted bed for decades, never dreaming she'd need this *procedure*. Her skin looks wan as dawn. Her sky-blue hospital gown, an awkwardly tied knot at the neck, rides up and parts. The gown looks like an out-sized cardigan sweater donned backwards in haste. If in fact it were a sweater, she might blush at her slight error, though I wouldn't see the blush: she lies well out of reach, her back to me.

The nurse says, "Look." Perhaps to distract me, she is pointing down at a bat, aimlessly circling over the cars that nose each other like a fattening herd in the lot below.

"Poor thing," I mutter, banally.

Something called white-nose fungus has decimated our bat population. A dazed few like this one take suicidally to air in winter. The window casements shudder and rattle. I'd never imagined this moment in this room, no, nor that we'd ever miss a summer evening's cloud of bats.

My wife's almost sixty, but her torso's long and graceful, her vertebrae make those dear, delicate nubs, the swell of her hip's still a marvel in my view. I'm waiting for whatever judgment her medical test will render, but there are stirrings within me, inappropriate and shameful, and so, to quell them, I watch the bat as it darts and flutters. I picture a cave every inch as empty as the one Mary of Magdala found: where bats once roosted, nothing but bleached excrement now.

My wife would let herself worry, tender-hearted as always, if she heard so much as a word about this single, disoriented flyer. I wouldn't mention the bat even if she could hear. She lies there lissome as a lioness, despite the children, all of them grown women and men today. They nearly tore that precious body apart as, unmedicated, she bore them. Of course, she's deeply medicated now, and mumbles cryptic questions and comments in series.

There's nothing for bats to find here in full sunlight, even in summer. It's noon right now, though ersatz dusk fills the room. My love's mumblings grow louder, and I'm startled by the rasp in her voice. No, I'm scared beyond speech.

The doctor arrives, thank God, with a good report on the test. My mortal wife doesn't hear her mortal husband pass it along.

Now the bat is clinging to the window ledge. Its frail wings barely twitch on the granite.

WORDSWORTH

My wife calls it my Wordsworth act. I seem more disposed to eulogize my youth than ever, though in truth I did so even at thirty. Like Wordsworth. But the great poet did so even younger, which better not mean that in my seventies I've become a rigid old fool. Like Wordsworth.

When I woke up today from a doze in this cabin I happened to notice a coat peg, and, still half-asleep, I addressed it out loud: "Goodbye," I said, as though I'd had my final slumber but one, and soon would lose that fine wry woman and our children forever, and that peg too, which unaccountably seemed to mean more than it should.

It felt sad to think ahead to people and places I'd have to surrender, because I'm still plenty thirsty for life, despite its aches both small and great: like my father gone too young, who used the peg for his silly Norfolk jacket, which even he hated. That's why he brought it to these wild back woods and waters, where it made even less sense than elsewhere.

And there our mother hung her sun hats, apparently unaware of how stupid or ugly they looked. She missed a lot by being so drunk so often. Still, she'll always be my only mother, and *de mortuis nihil nisi bonum*. My wife and I likewise have put things on the peg, things our children usually kept from making fun of as stupid or ugly, as they may have thought them. Of course they did: that's part of being anyone's son or daughter.

When he tapped the coat peg in, the sweat of my father's hand must have sunk into the whittled wood, which looks to be white cedar.

Senseless instinct can take a man over. Whatever else could make me want to lick that cedar and taste his salt, or to summon my mother back, the flask corked tight. I keep trying to have had a happy childhood. Just call me Wordsworth. With luck, you live to a lucky age. My father did not, and my mother lived on with ill fortune. I eulogize for twisted reasons.

Coat peg, I think, far too odically, you were important in your own small way. Will I get to tell you once again *Goodbye*, remembering you from among so many other things both great and small that will seem, the light closing down, to have been important after all?

BLUES FOR THE TENOR MAN

—*Washington, D.C., 2013*

HE MUST GUARD THAT TREASURE with a fierceness as great as his playing is masterful. I see it's a Selmer, top of the top of the line, Mark IV, the kind of sax he could pawn for several grand. His pants obviously belonged to somebody else at one time, their shredded cuffs risen to display a strange blue latticework of lesions on ashen shins.

The boxboard placard's scrawl is "HELP IM A HOMELESS VET."

I'd never have thought he smoked, and a pipe of all things. Wet and rough, its stem pokes out of his Navy pea coat's slash pocket. He's so good he makes some better part of me float to a long-closed club, Sonny Stitt jauntily trotting his horn through "The Sunny Side of the Street," which happens to be the song this poor vet offers above the tuneless traffic. He plays even this jump ballad so intensely I'd bet the flesh under his raveling watch cap must actually flinch.

I might of course recall the other Sonny, or the great Coltrane, or the under-prized Lucky Thompson. Herbie and I played them all in that student apartment where, kids that we were, we imagined ways to resolve the world's most un-accommodating problems, of which, at least to us, Racial Relations, as people said back then, were among the first.

We were children, true, but we worshiped the art that Roland Kirk had dubbed black classical music. And here's this tenor man, pushing me back to reverie and reverence, sliding now straight into a blues in a minor key, a number I don't know. Eyes clenched, he rocks and sways, the tenor, I'd swear, igniting the stars.

Blue pigeons drop from government marble, as if their tiny brains understood the mix of resolution and pain the music spreads around their strut. Their plumage seems to glow more warmly now, yet the damage that anyone's life can attract appears more clearly too, darkness cutting into light. That's the way of the blues.

To hand the tenor man a couple of dollars would somehow be to diminish us both. But what do I really know? I'm headed off for an expensive meal.

I wonder where Herbie lives now. The Lucky, the 'Trane, the Sonnys, and hundreds more were gems that he and I had gathered from hockshop and secondhand store, and they all were stolen one night. If only we'd kept up our guard, I think. If only we'd known how to hold onto what we treasured. How suddenly things can be taken, though a record collection is only a record collection.

Tonight the saxophonist will huddle beneath whatever wrappings he can gather against the cold, the noble Selmer, pearl of great price, clamped onto his chest with both hands as he sleeps. Or so I imagine.

As evening steals in, the horn moans an aching cadenza that ends the blues.

Commuters pour downward into the Metro, unhearing. The pigeons flap roostward. Soon there will be nothing for him to do but lie down with what he loves, under a bridge, in a shelter, wherever he may live.

SMELLY SOCKS: REVISION

9/11/2002

IF YOU'RE AN AUTHOR, some people seem to assume you instinctively know more than other people, even if a given subject involves things that, like so many, you don't have any answers for. The premise is absurd, of course, and yet—given the disruption to our national life in 2001—I figured some would be asking me, *How has this changed your life and work?* Or more simply: *What are your thoughts on the catastrophe?*

Indeed, some have asked me and still do, but these quick-fire twelve months later, I insist on answering, *I don't know.* Nor do I trust anyone who claims to. We'll all need time. In fact, probably what remains of any contemporary's life won't be adequate.

My thoughts, I suspect, are inconsequential at all events. But then so are those of the self-appointed sages, who believe, whatever the enormity, they can step right through it to the proper moral stance. I wonder how their phone calls might have sounded from an upper floor, while the jumpers jumped and some who had authority—deed not word—searched the Hadean stairwells, not looking for morals but mortals. How would the pundits sound right now if their native language were Arabic?

What actually strikes me at the moment is the smell of these socks I'm putting on for a hike, which should be washed but may never be, except by rain and the flow of the brooks where I ramble. That ammoniac odor calls to mind the one from my high school locker after football practice, which came at me as strong as furnace blast. Yet the stink somehow made me feel proud: it told me I was tough. I had survived.

At 8:36 this morning, the national Moment of Silence, at the exact spot on Route 5 where I was driving at that hour last year, having dropped our daughter at school, a child for whom I'd have laid down all my lives were I a cat, and would somewhere have found nine more for each of her sisters and brothers—at 8:36 I recalled how the girl had dressed herself in red, white, and blue that morning, a patriot by accident. She was fixed, thank God, on how she looked and not on what any big event could mean. She was ten. I did not ask her how her world had changed, though surely it had done so for her as much as for me, perhaps more.

This morning, I did not sob, or not quite, on hearing the names of victims recited over the air. I did suddenly feel American, however, far more than I had at the time of actual calamity, though I wonder what I mean by that. The feeling had to do with the north-country landscape, which has written itself all over me; it had something to do with my late father, a World War II veteran; something to do with the college roommate lost in Vietnam. It had something to do as well with the volunteer firemen who gathered silently at attention in my tiny town, wide spot in the road. I was almost home by then. How they moved me, pathetic creatures, people I knew one and all, and of course no more pathetic than you or I, than all of us in our feckless urge to do or utter whatever it is we'd give our souls for—or so we say.

And now, the hour of catastrophe marked and gone by, the names all read for the year, I pull on the smelly socks, take my staff in hand, and head out to storm the woods and hills in a fury of rage or love or something else, or many things. It's many things, no doubt.

I'm not tough. An odor merely recalls a time when I dreamed of being.

The first chill wind of fall comes crashing hard against me, trees' debris in the air, thick woods ablaze, my need today again evident, more so than ever, to revise and revise what I once thought I was and thought I'd be, and thought life amounted to, and nation. That need had always been there, of course, as it should be, and again will be, and surely again will be.

AMERICAN DREAM, 2004

*—for Marjan Strojan, after the second inauguration
of George W. Bush*

THE LITERARY SYMPOSIUM is over for the day. Wanting a bit of time to myself, I have come to this pleasant restaurant overlooking Lake Bled, that jewel of Slovenia.

The cuisine is also pleasant, somewhat Latin but something else too, which I can't find language to describe. A stone church guards a distant bluff and another guards the water's solitary island, which is in fact the only island in this small, lovely nation. I watch the wooden longboats full of tourists, rowed from abaft by men who lean and straighten, lean and straighten. It's a graceful movement, dance-like.

Here on the terrace there's actual dance: a woman singer, one man on Fender bass, another playing some sort of squeezebox, because there always seems to be a squeezebox in this part of the world. I suppose I'd call their music pleasant too. It finds some niche between exuberant techno-pop and the classical stuff derived from folksong, of which the middle-European composers have always been so fond.

There's an old-world melancholy here where I sit, for which I appear to be a sucker. The dancers mostly look thinner than they would in similar places back home. But then back home there *are* no similar places, really, no dancers who move as these do, with composure and flair at once. It's suddenly easy to dream of bolting my dear country and moving to somewhere like this, leaving behind the relative absence of style and civilization, the maddeningly insular frame of mind that doesn't even know there exists somewhere like this.

I'd flee all that *stuff*, like those muscle-bound trucks with their oversized US flag decals and their shark-mouth grilles. I'd flee 24-ounce steaks, TVs that reach the ceiling at Wal-Mart or Target or Circuit City.

I had wanted solitude, but it's likely I'm only lonely.

I have no local language. Yet I do have others. Maybe in time I'd make my way.

All at once, the three musicians play a different music, however awkwardly. The lake downhill remains a gemmy teardrop, and even through the tune I hear the gentle *tong* of the island's bell. The boatmen lean and row as deftly as they did before the mist and the evening settled in. I look but I can't see that slip of island.

First the band takes up "Last Date," all sweet and sour pap—unless like me you remember King Curtis's version on his soprano sax, glissandi flickering, wrenching. That tiny, hole-in-the-wall club. The late great King.

The trio slides unstopping into "Please Release Me." The pretty singer would kill to be Ray Charles. She fails. Who wouldn't?

I had those same two bluesy anthems in that same order on my big old pickup's scratchy tape deck thirty-odd years ago. My love and I, not quite man and wife yet, would creep after dark along the rut-and-gravel roads of our Vermont, notes spilling out the windows. Now I wonder if the thing we call coincidence is real? Be that as it may, I'm sick for home, which is what, if you look at its roots, nostalgia means.

We hung on each other close as summer air and sang along with those tunes. Deer peeled off our headlights, thick as mice, and August's moon looked as huge as we could ever dream.

GONE TO GRACE

—in memory of the Reverend Malcolm Grobe (1931-2013)

THE DAY BEFORE MALCOLM'S FUNERAL, I'd been talking with a blacksmith friend. He told me he'd recently spent some pretty hard hours with a pair of three-year-old Friesian mares who'd never had their feet trimmed. In that moment, I thought of a feral donkey in Ireland, back three decades: poor animal, lowly mount of the Christ, hobbling on hooves long as bread loaves. These things had nothing whatever to do with Malcolm, except they did.

He was the one who pronounced us husband and wife. It seemed a wonder then, still does. I'd gotten the girl, which shocked me, the way it does the star-struck hero in sappy movies. In any case, Malcolm is part of a long, joyful marriage, and the family it made, including the ones he baptized.

One reading came from a funny note he'd left for the pastor, which said in part: "Beware! Non-judgment day is coming." I could virtually *feel* Malcolm's voice, insisting as ever that God was too big to conform to anyone's will. There was no one so evil or sick, he claimed, as to be beyond the Lord's grace.

The man was frumpy and funny but mostly just good. He was an improbably accomplished athlete as well, and improbably fierce on the courts, no matter he loved his every opponent. In keeping with his wishes, his ashes were interred in a tennis-ball can.

It may seem bizarre that I conjured horse or donkey just then, but later, as we mourners chuckled and wept, I imagined I heard soft words. They were Malcolm's, whose hand would surely have stroked those neglected, suffering creatures.

That funeral day, for so many there, was painful enough I'd almost swear it hurt them to stand on God's green earth.

For my part at least, I wished I could somehow walk a little while on air.

RECOMPENSE

A GROWN BALD EAGLE FLEW out from the eastern shore of
Molly's Falls Pond, the bird's white extremities all the whiter
for the sun, whose dome had just now shown. I felt pleased
enough by this grace, though it was a minor one these days,
the eagles so well recovered.

And then, my mind being still, for worse or better, the
only mind I own, the moment was crossed by instinctual let-
down: there, I thought, goes one more wonder that in older
age is a good deal less wondrous than once.

My inexcusable mopery did not deserve the next turn,
unless somehow, somewhere I had favored someone with
kindness. How else except as a form of reward should I of
all people be granted witness to that other bird, up higher,
which suddenly dwarfed the bald one, whose ivory head and
tail now paled? What generous fate could have brought a
view of those awful wings, which moved in a way to which
the flat verb *flap* could never be adequate? To me in fact the
physics of that flight showed something near anti-motion.
Imperiously lazy, how could the motion keep that phenome-
nal frame suspended?

A golden eagle in Vermont.

A bright patina lay on the water. From that exact moment, my languorous paddle spilled long seams of silver,
the hills around the lake shone blue, a pair of trout rose and
rolled on the surface, making a lustrous froth.

That breathtaking bird, which enthusiasts east of the Mississippi so avidly seek, and skillfully, sometimes for decades—why should I be blessed to behold it as I dawdled on the water, dodging the horrid heat that had held for five days straight?

I suddenly understood, or thought at least I did, that the noblest kindness is the one you may have offered all unconsciously. Did some mysterious higher power feel I'd done some good? Or that I'd mourned enough for a while, my dear student Matthew dead, my Uncle Peter, and now Annie Fitch, my kids' honorary grandmother? There had been this late welter of crushing disappearances: I'd lamented them, of course, but remained as full of questions as of tears. Why was I still hardy? Why did I have no knee or hip or shoulder that needed attention? No stammering heart. No traitorous joint or tendon. No cancer like what some beloved friends were fighting: I thought of Chip and Billy, younger men for whom I've long felt such love, however insufficient my expression of it.

Soon things began to stir: a scolding jay, a ragged crowd of ravens gawping, a log truck downshifting on the far road where I'd parked. A muggy wind rose up to flick leaves in the hardwood forest out of listlessness, a far dog yipped, two campers left their tent to clatter sooted cookware. And yet to watch the golden eagle's lordly drifting out of sight was unaccountably to hope that in my own small life I'd shown a kindness or two to people. How else, again, to explain this odd compensation?

Comedy

GOUT

I'd stood by the pond on that early-winter morning,
new snow lying on its ice. I once again acknowledged the gal-
lop of time, but also warmed to the notion of repetition: another year, another gilding of things by natural wonder, and I
a more than lucky witness.

I stood again later, this time in my living room, and suffered a stab through my foot as if from a knife—no, more
surprising, as if I'd unwittingly stepped on a nail. I hopped
over to a chair, but for hours could feel no relief, so at last,
reluctantly, I traveled downriver to the clinic, my good wife at
the wheel. I'd wait there for many more hours still.

At 3 A.M., the doctor announced, "It's gout."

Gout? Isn't that something for jowly old men at their
port, I wondered? I was thinking of accounts I'd read of Tory
poets and their circles. And to think that at dawn I'd been
nearly gloating over my own bodily condition, vain of the
mountain hikes I still could take, despite my seven decades.

Early next morning I woke pain-free, as though not a
thing had happened, and plunged into the woods again as
I had for God knows how many mornings before, noticing
how the fog of the prior evening had frozen into lace on each
tree in the forest, every branch brilliant as gemstone. I'd lost
any inkling of discomfort, not to mention disaster.

It was good to be out right now, because the radio's
weather report for the next day predicted snow and rain at
once, a nasty mix.

CAMP BY THE RIVER

THERE SHOULD BE SNOW—there always used to be—but the ground's still bare here well beyond Thanksgiving, which allows me to find the oak leaf. In my seventy years, I've never seen one half so big, although it dropped from a tree whose trunk is a mere foot around, child of the huge oak next to the river, which has stood intact, or mostly, through decades of storm. The big tree's acorns fall to water, making perfect, momentary circles, like dimpling fish.

I should pick up the outsized leaf and put it between waxed paper sheets, then iron it flat, because I may never see its like again. The wind heaves in from north, and could blow it out of sight.

An eagle coasts downstream, the way an eagle will, come early winter. I've seen that bird, or others like him, all my life. He scatters some black ducks, who race for shelter under the cutbanks. Perhaps I feel what I feel for being here alone. Last night the moon stared through the same old pine, and now red squirrels tease my dog from the very tree that gave up the giant leaf.

I used to laugh at such doggy antics with Earl, old river-driver, who'd often come to visit back then. I treasured all his stories of times when his crew moved logs by water. The squirrels were different, the hunting dog too, even the grand oak. *Another time, another place,* as Earl liked to say. The neighborhood has changed, subtly in some ways, radically in others, and Earl has disappeared.

No metaphoric sighing on the page, I think. Yet I still don't know how I'll ever leave this place, or leave my children and their children, or the wife who's stood by me no matter.

I could prop the leaf on the table by the window through which I now consider the things I consider. I think it again: the leaf could disappear in this huffing north wind. I guess I'll let it. Even if I preserved the thing, it could never be a monument, could never hold a trace of what this cabin and the gregarious flesh it has sheltered have been for me.

SAY WHEN:
A DECEMBER LITANY

TO MYSELF I SAY, *Say When,* though that seems unlikely. It'll never be time for me to say that. To say it would demand that I grow tired, for instance, of climbing the shaled, sprucey ridges of northern New England. I'd have to tire of the first real snow of winter, of the beast-tracks in it that so fascinate me. The winter-gouged outline of Mt. Moosilauke, off to our east, would no longer quicken my spirit but cause it to chill like this December dawn.

I could only say when when joy and hope no longer quelled my petty emotional rumpuses—nerves, for example, in the small hours of morning. I might say when if I no longer felt a glow as I thought forward to family at a Christmas reunion, little ones roaring around the house, the kitchen woodstove humming with scarlet heat as the temperature outdoors fell below zero, our supper steaming in that room, in that house, in those woods, a kitchen become the soul of light.

And the words of brilliant authors, both dead and living, would have to lie flat on the page, never rising to dance like the ghost of an Irishman on his coffin at a wake, where fellowship and cheer and love should prevail. I could no longer read those writers' pages until sleep supervened and I fell into sweet dreaming, despite the politicians' and homicides' and greed-mongers' rule of the news.

I might say when if life no longer felt, precisely, like a lucky dream for me and when I didn't know anymore how to thank the God of my understanding for it. I would have constantly and not just occasionally to surmise that these people sitting around me in our village's china-white, trim, and resonant Congregational chapel were perhaps deluded fools, and I too, and that it was, precisely, delusion to praise such a soul as Edee's or Ralph's or Marion's or David's. I'd have to imagine that their abundant goodness, unknown to the wide, brute world, meant nothing whatever as the rulers of that world pursued their acquisitions and wielded their powers, while those who have lost all powers and possessions lay shivering in cardboard boxes or bombed alleys.

My wonderful, bounding pointer bird dog would no longer dazzle and delight as he rambled along the countryside with me; his musculature and movements no longer simple marvels, or not so simple, and I wouldn't therefore huff a cloud into thin air which lazed up a sidehill and then quickly faded, as if that spurt of breath symbolized something gloomily evanescent, when in truth the cloudlet would only blend, as it always has, with the brightness of a day—one like this in the month of my birth, Capricornus, when I'm blessed to wander this small and infinite planet.

FOR DONALD AND JOHN

MY FRIEND JOHN THE BLACKSMITH lent me an old book by Donald Culross Peattie, *A Natural History of North American Trees*. The volume is both quaint and authoritative, and it may be this combination of qualities that caused John, as he handed it to me, to call it "perfect."

When I got home, I turned to the chapter on the hop hornbeam, a tree I've always treasured, although I've never really figured out why. After all, it's a killing wood to chop or work, as I've often proved to myself. No wonder its folk names are ones like *ironwood* or *lever-wood*.

Mr. Peattie muses that "everything about this little tree is at once serviceable and self-effacing. Such members of any society are easily overlooked, but well worth knowing." I looked up from that passage and thought of the blacksmith himself; he's a bright man, but reticent—and tough as hornbeam. And I thought, so to speak, *through* John to a long gone friend, Don Chambers, who once cut that wood all through a long winter. Back in his time, before the arrival of synthetics, its rigid, tight-grained lumber was used for stretcher and coffin handles. I recall Don's telling me, "By God, you didn't want *them* loads to tumble."

Illness and death called on the lever-wood's strengths, so it may appear odd for me to make of this scurfy tree a token of life and health. But who's going to notice, really?

And can't I anyhow forge some empowering symbol from the tree's fruit, which stands on the branch right through winter, a browse for deer and grouse and whatever else may seek it? Perhaps searching for another sort of nurture, I've now and then plucked some of those florets to lay on my desk, for however brief a time, as if to put them there in the bitter-coldest months might also help sustain a household.

I once used five cord of ironwood to heat our house through a winter, having left the logs unsplit. My maul couldn't crack them, and when I tried the wedge, I buried it in the heartwood of one stout log, no way to fetch it back but to burn the log and pull the out of the fire, as John does a shoe.

I smile as I picture John when he handed me his book. He was dressed as always in greens, his beard swept sideways to his face from laying a cheek against the flank of a horse, I suspect. Though he owns a small herd of Suffolk Punch for his own pleasure, he doesn't make a living putting shoes on working stock these days as much as on fancy saddle horses. Things change. In my mind's eye, he has shaped the shoe on his forge and plunged it deep into the bucket of hissing water, and now he's nailing it fast.

I've lived my life by words for the most part and somehow been more recognized for that than I'd ever have imagined. Suddenly I'm my beloved state's poet laureate, a post that thrills and humbles me at once. There could easily and justifiably have been another selected for the post. I've been talking and talking and talking, writing and writing and writing, more than ever. So as I imagine two terse men with entirely different ways to navigate the world, steady ones who've made more palpable gestures than any of mine, I get an odd feeling, or perhaps—no, definitely—a mixture of feelings. I'd surely be wrong to define what I feel as simple envy. It's better than that. Is it love, or admiration, or both? Doubtless it's both, along with other responses less easy to name.

I picture John holding nails in his teeth and whispering past them, not to a saddle horse but to a great blond Belgian gelding. The hoof before him stretches wide as an old-time privy hole. And, under a sky so blue it's really some other color, also beyond description, Don still drives his saw through ironwood, skidded to roadside by just such a draft horse. His wire spectacles glint in January's sun. Even through his plaid mackinaw, I can see the cannonball biceps on his short arms. If he took off his chopper's mitts to greet me, I'd feel the calluses of decades in the north woods.

It would be a good thing, I surmise, to let these good and honest men direct me to the end of the day, or at least to the end of these thoughts.

In another era, this might be the point at which the author addressed his gentle reader, tacking on a moral of some sort. And since I am, precisely, summoning two figures from another era, I'll go ahead and offer the address, minus the moral, because I can't say what that could possibly be.

Reader, perhaps you will tell me that these things and people and labors that so obsess me are worth nobody's notice in our time, that I'm only sentimental, that the best thing I could do would be to write a poem, a not untypical elegy, or even a book of poems about all such matters. Even if I did, of course, it would scarcely be what John calls a perfect book. That's beyond my reach, even if perfection might be possible for a blacksmith, or for a dear old lumberjack, the one who—along with the farrier—started me thinking this way in the first place.

FLOATERS AND FLASHERS

I WAS BUSTING MY GUT IN A KAYAK, just a manic old man shooting across the bow of time, attempting to hold five-plus miles per hour for an hour.

What had seemed at first a hair rankled me, flitting across my sight while I paddled. I kept brushing at it now and then with the back of my starboard hand as I stroked, but it stayed, all the way upstream and down.

It turned out not to be a hair but what's called a floater. In bed that night, I also detected silver flash after flash at the corners of my eyes, all that glint and glimmer perhaps like the visions some of us sought for in mescaline back in the '60s. I was among the seekers.

It's been a long spell since I craved altered states or so-called trips—except of course for ones along my river, whose every armlet and bend feel familiar to me as home. So do its grackles and warblers, skipping among the streamside trees, all its hordes of insects hatching, its herons and ducks, its mink and muskrat and beaver.

My doctor worried mildly about my retina, and set up an appointment next day with an ophthalmologist. I dreamed myself blind as a cave fish all through an overnight of damp, tormented sleep. But next morning the specialist assured me my eyes looked fine for someone over sixty, and I was a fair way over. A cataract had started, too, but there'd likely be no surgery for a few more years, praise be.

You live a while and things begin to happen. Strange, small impairments come and go and come again: maybe for instance a finger welds itself to your palm and aches, but then it loosens again—until it comes back, the body's simulacrum of a moment, say, when you may have caused a child to cry, a moment he or she has likely gotten over in adulthood. You may forget it yourself for decades, but it has never truly disappeared at all.

If I can deploy so much will in wielding a paddle for scores and scores of minutes, thrashing the surface this way, why not exercise as much on my frame of mind? I try it, thinking I can choose to be stirred by that osprey, say, which drops from that tall red oak. He almost hovers, then gently floats downriver, dihedral of wings as clear as day.

I vow to be done with painful recall, to act just now at least as though I've never known a thing about melancholy. I scan the shallows, grateful to see, above their shadows, the scurry of minuscule fish in their schools.

Silver flash after flash.

THE HOST IN MY DENTURES

Plock!

It was rim-shot-loud, the puck that struck my mouth; in fact, the sound impressed me much more than the pain. At first, that is.

Five decades having passed, I'm wearing the partial bridge that came of that moment. Not that all my top teeth were knocked out; truth is, the two most affected were simply loosened for a while. My mother didn't think I needed a dentist. "They'll firm up again in time," she ventured.

My mother imagined me tough as she was. I wasn't. I'm not.

"Things pass," she said. They didn't.

Of course the fault lay partly with me. At sixteen. I didn't wear helmet or mask, because my teammates and I all thought—I use the verb "to think" a bit loosely—that we'd skate right over any wound. That sort of protection was not for genuine men, which we all were aiming to be.

I suffered as much from resentment as from anything physical. I should have been hurt in a game at least, not practice! The shot had burst off Bill Chadford's stick and caught me as I knelt on the rink to block it.

Kneeling this morning, I took the cup and the bread, and yet I felt a certain dreariness come upon me. This much later, I still feel scraps of the Host in my dentures. They start me thinking back, even as I should still be thinking of the present, the presence.

I remember my girlfriend Constance sitting up in the bleachers that evening. Because, as I say, what she watched was only practice, she likely felt bored stiff, though now I can't be certain she didn't feel equally so when I played in actual games.

I'd been glancing her way and smiling as brightly as I knew how, ever since taking the ice. I meant to let her know how centrally she figured into my thoughts, even as I rushed up and down the ice. I particularly wanted to get a knock-out shoulder check into Chadford, who'd been her boyfriend before me. Idiot adolescent male logic: if I could set him on his rear end, I figured, she'd see just how right a choice she'd made, swapping sissy for bruiser. But Fate didn't like me, it seemed, Chadford himself the one who whacked me in the face. He *would* be.

Even stanching my face with a sleeve as I skated to the sideboards, I took note of Constance's classic features, her perfect hair, her sweet breath that had crystallized and settled as powder on the shoulders of the letter sweater I'd given her less than a month before.

Less than a month after, I'd have the sweater back. She was too flawless to keep.

As for me, I'd keep my teeth—but only until age began to catch up and that ancient disaster, which had bloomed in my roots, played itself again, tooth after tooth, six in all, going gray and at last coming out. The dreariness that fell upon me today in church went back perhaps to that girl, to how she quit me, and abruptly. And now who would love a dark-mouthed geezer? So I asked myself as I sat back in the pew, which was inexcusable coming from a man more happily married than anyone merits.

Nonetheless, I asked it: Who will love me? I knew full well what I ought to answer in that place and time: God. But the very word stuck in my maw, even after communion, which is meant after all to change our view of the world, of ourselves and our fellow humans.

I wasn't worthy, I was. I'm not, I am.

These hours later, I call back that *plock*, but at last something roughly like thought supervenes: *These are the teeth of my body, broken for Thee*, I mutter, perhaps blasphemously. They were not broken for Constance, or Ginnie or Peg or Patty or Bea. They were broken for no other heartbreak love of my young manhood.

Having no choice, I decide to take some satisfaction in bearing these orts, lodged in the wire-and-plastic contraption, through another day.

O saving remnants.

SEAMS SEW EASY

—in mem. Ruth Day Bean
(1919-2004)

A DAY BEFORE SHE PASSED, Ruthie told us she'd tried to telephone but couldn't see to punch the buttons. It was doubtless her glaucoma, known to her as *galcoma*, just as another ailment—one of the many—was *emsemo*. She hadn't been able to breathe, she was scared, she wanted to call "because I felt just as though I was going to die." And she wanted to see her soldier nephew Leon, home on leave from what she called *Juaq*.

Oh, those neologisms! The *Aridonnick* Mountains, the *plascit* bags, and once—a mystery she took to her grave—an aching wrist, which she claimed, her longtime doctor had called *a ruffled lotus*.

Then Ruth did die, and the world seemed badly other without this valiant woman, after all our years of loving her, no matter we laughed behind her back—at her macular degeneration, for further instance, which by way of her verbal alchemy turned into *immaculate de-odination*.

Use your fingers, your unruffled fingers, to count how few there may have been in your life as in ours of whom it may be said what we said of Ruth: "She didn't have a mean bone in her body." Or: "She never breathed an evil word about anyone." But all that was true of Ruthie, who even prayed for those ravening vultures from the fuel company who stole from her government heating assistance until my lawyer wife ran them out of the state.

You could say those things about her, a woman who cared for each of our sons and daughters off and on for decades. And the kids, from the firstborn man to the twelve-year-old child wondered, too, at a Ruthless world, and we all wept together as one in the pew, and I thought how good this sadness was, how much we loved her, how real the sadness felt. It was ours and we'd save it.

We'd do all that, and so we'd save dear Ruthie forever too, who no longer need feel more nor less safe than she did, if she did, for the overthrow of some dictator out in Juaq. And when it fell, the last bit of earth, that savvy wife looked to me more lovely, and the children more dear and fine.

Later I drove the youngest to Woodsville, to "Seams Sew Easy," the fabric and sewing shop in that hardscrabble town where once, an elderly neighbor has told me, forty trains arrived each day, and the mills were active, and there was no ugly big box store or Dunkin Donuts, and no notions shop would ever have been given so corny a name.

The girl wanted to make herself a simple skirt, her first, and the woman who minded the store was patient and kind. I killed some time by the smutted window, looking out as the sunlight of early spring or late winter, whatever you'd want to call it, shied off the grim granite storefronts.

And while I was woolgathering, that decent woman guided our daughter, fingering the cloths and laying them out so that their beautiful, colorful patterns showed clearly.

Coming back to myself, I thought a plain thought. With the deep-down, *formal* ease that comes, as wondrous Emily Dickinson writes, after great pain, and with the ammoniac odor of weeping still in my head, I thought, *This life's all right.*

SURVIVING ROMANCE

THE WORLD SWELTERS, even at twilight on this August Sunday. My great love naps, her hair lank and humid across her forehead. The blunt protrusion of an empty wine bottle from last night's party, which all day we have forgotten to clear away, bobs above the scratched rim of a bucket, its ice long gone liquid. How tempting it is for me to laze here too in the dank present.

"It must be jelly, 'cause jam don't shake like that." Big Joe Turner's figuration from my ancient turntable, the volume low, recalls not some erotic encounter but a dawn from years and years ago, which might seem to urge, *Hurry back.* I remember mornings then, the streets' tar not yet a-shimmer with heat. Our family was passing two weeks in a rented seaside cottage.

Just a little boy, I'd race every day to the tide-washed beach to gather jellyfish, which lay bright as jewels in the sand—perfect, intact. I'd carry them home in a bucket, store them down-cellar until dark, then haul them up at about this very hour, stashing them under my bed. It made no sense, except that it did, to me.

Just under y bedroom's floor, each night I'd hear my father rocking my mother in the bamboo glider. Soon, suddenly and mysteriously, their lively chatter subsided to indecipherable whispers. My crisp sheets wilted; cicadas droned; headlights circuited the walls.

While I slept, those parents drained my treasures into a canal beside the house. I wouldn't learn they had done that until much later. It seems that the stench from the pail grew pretty awful by ten o'clock. They'd fill the bucket with water from that rank canal, explaining how jellyfish dissolve once they're out of the sea.

An inexcusable lie, I suppose, but a dispiriting one. Every day, the same dreary routine: dissolution, vanished particularity. It all seemed tragic but unavoidable.

Since then, as for anyone, of course, experience has leached the glitter from other ruses as well. I have at times responded to all that with the same old disenchantment, as if most of what we men and women value will always trickle back to a native, general ocean. One assembles hopes or objects or affections or memories—and they all dissolve.

Yet some things are not so fugitive after all. I note the gray in my wife's full hair, the slack of her jaw as she slumbers, and each appears a feature of the most beautiful creature I've ever imagined. Her length of limb and neck strike me as nigh miraculous.

My senses stir: a breeze comes in, stiffening from northwest now, and the day's stifling vapor lifts. Outdoors, there is no miasma of mudflat, teeming canal, old fish; I hear no soporific hum of tires on pavement; I whiff the spice of evergreen, the deeper one of dark earth; the comical drone of a bullfrog reaches me from the pond.

I'd felt as though my very flesh were liquefied. Now, as that gathering wind caresses the curtains and my sweat dries, I stand and put a match to a candle on the table. Its slight flame leans inward. I imagine sharp stars. My love's ring-gems glitter in the subtle light, as drops might on a window screen after rain. She seems a girl in such illumination; her eyes have that star-like glitter too, familiar and dear, as she wakes and smiles.

TRANSFIGURATIONS

—Bow River, Alberta

THE ROWDY GULLS seemed willfully derisive creatures. Their yammer prompted instantaneous anger in me, crescendoing as they did just after my mammoth trout threw the hook.

That was the fish I'd traveled here for, and I'd drawn it so close that each haloed spot showed clear to my eye, even though the river had turned murky, its surface pocked by storm. The feral self of my young manhood returned, as if it had never been gone—which I suppose it hadn't altogether. Incredibly, it appeared to me, a man of over seventy, that what remained of my life would come to nothing.

My brother rocked in the bow of the drift boat we'd rented. He'd caught his own trophy minutes before, and released it. Now he teased me and, incredibly, in that instant he seemed my enemy. What madness could *that* have been?

In due course reason came back, so that I could weigh such insignificant loss against the loss of loved ones to age or disease. I likewise considered my luck in my brother's beloved company, and in observing the elegant downstream bend in the river, above which a pair of ospreys teetered on spruce limbs.

It was in that very moment, suddenly serene, that I missed my wife, my grownup children, a grandchild who liked to invent games for me, her younger brother, I hoped, waiting his turn to do the same, and his twin cousins too.

Ineffable changes came along with an effortless dawdle of snow, through which the sun now angled down to the river.

My trout was already cached in memory's vaults. The squalling gulls showed angel-pale. I turned and smiled at my brother, whom I'd treasured all his life. He smiled back.

And all was well. And all manner of thing was well.

CURRENT

—in mem. Strachan Donnelly

IT'S A LATE AFTERNOON just after Labor Day, and I'm paddling, or rather drifting, five miles downriver. I know each yard of this lazy, unruffled stretch. I've already passed what I call Deerfly Point, for the whining greenhead pests that seem always to dart out and storm me there. The flies are drawn to my bald head, which I never have the sense to cover, thirsty as I am for breeze and sun to touch any piece of me that can feel them. And just now I'm approaching a spot I've named Black Duck Beach, a flat gone broad with autumn, where scores of the ducks assemble before the hunters' season; the bright, Indian Summer sun has lacquered them there, immobile.

But tomorrow will find me in New York City, among a crowd commemorating a friend of almost fifty years. Most of us mourners have reached a point where we'll be attending more burials than weddings from here on. I'm sure that's what has me musing this way.

Think of better things. I remember that advice from my mother when I was only a child, in some state of despondency or other. Maybe I know what it means now, though once that counsel made me furious. You can't just change a mood, I thought.

There would follow a long stretch anyhow, from late adolescence into early middle age, when I wanted to keep my mind *off* mere things, good or bad, meaning to concentrate on the rarefied, the abstract. Perhaps that's a trait of anyone's younger years. Today it feels respectful to exult, precisely, in specifics as I move along. It's something that my departed, outdoor-loving friend always did.

Those better particulars include the blue September day itself, in which I behold a cloud of early juncos, a daytime owl, pond-lilies glowing golder than they did all summer. South of me, a blue heron labors to get airborne, but when it succeeds, what grace there is in its slow winging. Will it alight around some downstream bend? I'll keep on drifting, hoping to find it whenever I reach such a turn. This sort of hope will keep me moving on. But in fact the current will do that on its own.

I look astern to something even more commonplace: the drops that trickle off the paddle with every stroke, forming a ragged, bright band behind me on the surface. A breeze lisps through the cottonwood, ash, and silver maple. The drops falling from the paddle make me suddenly think, *I'm on the water.* I'm not sure why, but that stuns, appears a sort of revelation. All these years I've come here to the river on as many warm days as I could, but now—perhaps because of the water's kinship to these few silent tears I hadn't even known were there—plain water has become a miracle.

I fight to clear my sight as I bob toward a bend. Maybe around it I'll flush the heron from tree or shore, but any wondrous, daily thing will do.

COMEDY: SUNSET POINT

I STAND BEFORE THE TREE, one pine with one especially graceful drooping branch that commands one edge of one island where our family cabin sits. It is exactly here that generations of children have been photographed, cradled by their elders in infancy, and then on their own as they stand and, year by year, they lengthen.

Farm Cove's evergreen muffin of mountain pops up, far in the distance; it's a background blur in those pictures. Closer by, water is brightened by westering suns. Now and then a loon sculls on the lake, or a tern flits up higher, or an eagle crosses clouds that seem lit from within.

In view of all this, I don't think I embarrass myself to claim that if there remains for my clan any sacred place, I'm in and on and under it as I stand by the pine.

The older the sons and daughters get, the smaller the mountain, though after all it was only the flatness of landscape that ever made something called *mountain* of that small hill. And Sunset Point is no point at all, properly speaking, but a rounded and rather short protrusion. Still, it does point to our longtime presence together.

Today, however, I'm here on my own. As if to remind me of that, not a bird appears, no wind stirs, and the further ground is gray all over in undistinguished weather. The sun of course will fall down if I watch it or don't, things slowly going dark, and even though I know I shouldn't, how easy for me to hitch my progress or rather declension to what I see or don't.

One brother is twenty-five years gone. If you live a while, there's undercurrent. All the elders are gone, but none of my generation's mothers is lost, nor I as yet, nor, praise be, any children. I must remind myself of that, must make my way to something like serenity. That seems an obligation. So I search within the framing tree not merely for what has been but also for what lingers within my reach, including this memory of our youngest, not even a teenager then. She's the family wit, who used to affect a gun moll's speech for comic purposes.

I told her I'd read that most poets are dead within a few years of my age. I admit I shivered slightly.

"Who?" she asked.

"Poets," I repeated.

"Well," she growled, "you got nothin' to worry about."

As I recall those words, I feel my worries soften, and when I stare into the empty embrace of the same old stooping pine, a laughter comes upon me, which, although it wouldn't and couldn't find its way into a snapshot, enlivens the sky, props up the mountain, beckons lively birds and a freshening wind as it rises above a long-loved island.

RIVER, STARS,
AND BLESSED FAILURE

I PAUSE IN MY DRIVE BACK HOME from a reading, un-
knotting my legs and back, which have stiffened while I've sat
at the wheel. It's a joy to behold the moon as it breaches the
mountain, though I feel even slighter than one of the beads
of froth down there in the rapids, which are winking back
at more stars than I've ever seen in New England. How can
there be so many? They rob my breath and speech.

I could almost read my poems out loud again by that
moon and those stars. But I'm not in the least inclined to do
that. I'm banishing words for the moment, as if by strange
instinct—not just my own words, but all. I find it more than
peaceful out here to articulate nothing, to feel myself on the
farthest edge of conscious thought.

Over the river's crackle, I catch the lyrical calling of a
coyote, and from it can imagine ones nearer to home, their
sopranos mixed with the altos of owls and the lilting descant
of a freshet. I picture my wife in our house. Perhaps she paus-
es by a certain window just now, the big one through which
at this time of year we watch the deer glide in to browse our
night-black lawn. Against that darkness, their bodies show
ashen, ghostly, elegant.

Our children are all grown and gone. And yet in this moment their distance feels slight. No longer are we at the exact

center of a family constellation, but even so—or is it there-fore?—we still know this thing we crudely call joy.

Of course, as one who always longs for the freshest and rarest expression of feeling he can muster, I might easily wince at so paltry and common a noun as that—*joy* indeed!—if I didn't find this a time, precisely, for rhetorical failure, no words quite apt for what shimmers out there above any one person's construals of meaning

CODA: THANK YOU NOTE

—Newbury Burial Ground, 2013

My wife says we'll be eternally close to Tink and Polly, old-time Vermonters, that vanishing stock, and best of neighbors. To me, she seems like some madwoman, talking about how we should stipulate a bench instead of a headstone to stand at this grave she bought yesterday, when I was out of town. A bench, she explains, will enable our children and grandchildren to sit, have picnics, enjoy the scenery. As they take in the panorama, she adds, they can think of us, and in this setting their thoughts will necessarily be happy ones.

Now I'll admit she's always been uncannily good at knowing what our children, and now their children, may need or want, but I'm skeptical of this rosy vision of hers. Our kids aren't as needy as many I've known in any case. Even when they were small, they often proved delightfully resourceful.

The two youngest daughters dreamed up sisters for their games: Sharlee was the bright one, Sally the drunken fool. They had Bunnum the rabbit too, and the younger girl often took on the role of Moodyhawk, an odd, mean character who claimed to rule the world. She came, as I recall, from Guam.

An older brother conceived and played the part of a dog named Ruffy. He would school his father or his mother, or often both at once, in their lines of dialogue with Ruffy, often scolding us for faulty inflection or body language. "Not like that!" he'd snap. (When he became a teenager, his grief at the death of his real dog, a sweet Labrador bitch called Plum, would keep him home from school one day.)

The eldest daughter, at four years old, reported, lisping the plural, that she'd found two slugs on a pumpkin. There was gusto, even mirth, in her description of how the orange of the mollusks and the orange of the fruit "didn't go together." She was visibly disappointed when she led me out to the garden; she couldn't find the slugs themselves, merely the pale paths they had left on descending and heading who knew where?

The firstborn child was obsessed with Jeeps, and in bumbling, nightly drawing lessons, I guided his hand with my own in our cold old kitchen. He'd whistle between his teeth in concentration, his breaths turning to small clouds in that frigid space, no matter the ancient Round Oak woodstove glowed red in the corner. Draft after draft after draft. He wanted perfection. Who doesn't long for that?

Standing on my grave, I start mourning, because I'll lose these moments and others accrued over so many years. In short, my own vision is far less cheery than my wife's. Is this a matter of gender? I'll never know. I can't speak for motherhood. But can anyone have been a father and conjured such random memories without some inward weeping?

Now, from the plot she's just bought, my wife sweeps an arm at the view again: looming above all else, there's our favorite mountain to eastward, purple with May but still holding snow at the summit. An eagle appears before it as if the woman had willed it there, the bird's reflection complete in the river's languid oxbow. Sun-spangled, it skims the treeline along the near shore. My love claps hands in witness, eyes joyous.

Meanwhile, and as always for no palpable reason, my mind makes its oblique jumps. I suddenly think of a check I left this morning for a woman who comes now and then to clean house. She bore a child in her teens, and might have gone on to harm, misery, or dependence; but her boyfriend stood by her, married her, helped her to raise that daughter. I admire that woman greatly: her industry, her constantly upbeat mood, whatever a given day's circumstances and despite her rheumatoid arthritis. I scribbled a thank you note to her along with the payment. Typically broody, I think just now how the note resembles so much I've put my hand to: a note is no more than a note, and still it's one more thing that will disappear for good.

Those children's children: how could I ever have known how much I'd love them? You see, it's not the abstraction death that daunts me; it's the leaving behind of all the beloved, particular creatures with whom I've walked the earth that will cover my ashes, and all the places on earth that have proved so dear to us. And yet my wife—without saying a word—reminds me that an apter feeling might be gratitude. I have had so much to lose in the first place.

I should study that. Maybe the bench is a fine idea after all.

ACKNOWLEDGMENTS

Many of these small essays first appeared in the following publications, sometimes with different titles, and sometimes in different, indeed radically different, forms:

Artful Dodge: "Dizzy"
Bloodroot: "Did He Think"
Brevity: "One More Eulogy"
Brilliant Corners: "The Touch," "My Time Machine," "I Listen to Some Blues," "Blues for the Tenor Man," "Mannish Boy"
The Café Review: "Micah, Weeping"
The Christian Century: "Gone to Grace," "Transfigurations," "Towards Easter, 2008: Eye on the Sparrow"
Connotation: "Outsider," "Same Old Path," "Old Country Song"
The Connecticut Review: "Stone Rollers," "The Beast in the Jungle," "Passing the Arts & Crafts Festival," "A Christian"
Connecticut Watershed: "Comedy: Sunset Point"
Gray's Sporting Journal: "Camp by the River," "Mickey," "I've Kept On Anyhow"
Great River Review: "Big Musquash Stream"
Hippocampus: "American Dream"
Hot Metal Bridge: "Jerry, Solitary," "Woman and Dog," "Jake in Circles"
The Hudson Review: "County Home: An Iraqui Suite," "Floaters and Flashers," "Seams Sew Easy"

Hunger Mountain: "Dejection in Late Winter"

Image: "Our Heads Against the Walls," "The Host in My Dentures," "Smitty's Not Right"

The Iowa Review: "Adolescence"

Measure: "Gout"

Mid-American Review: "Whatever I Might Say"

New Ohio Review: "Misterioso," "The Usual Way," "Whatever I Might Say"

Northern Woodlands: "For Donald and John"

Numéro Cinq: "Sex and Death," "Mrs. Ragnetti and the Spider," "Short Sad Story," "Catch," "The Couple at the Free Pile," "The Serpent on Barnet Knoll," "River, Stars, and Blessed Failure," "Thank You Note"

Passages North: "Recovery Room"

Poetryzoo: "The Big Idea"

River Teeth: "Black Marks"

Salmagundi: "Fools Day"

St. Petersburg Review: "Wordsworth"

Splash of Red: "Maya"

storySouth: "What's the Story?"

Tar River Poetry: "Current"

The Salon: "Have I Thought?"

TravelTainted: "Smelly Socks," "Surviving Romance," "Lame and Sound," "Maya," "Forgiveness," "Passing the Arts and Crafts Festival"

Writer's Chronicle: "How About Some Quiet In This Place?"

CPSIA information can be obtained at www.ICGtesting.com
Printed in the USA
LVOW10s0451161015

458519LV00006B/7/P